Understanding the Bible

Simply Understanding
the Bible

Irving L Jensen

CLF, Worthing
CLC, Alresford

© 1990 Irving L. Jensen

First published in the USA by
World Wide Publications, 1303 Hennepin Ave, Minneapolis,
Minnesota 55403, USA. A publishing ministry of the
Billy Graham Evangelistic Association.

First British edition published 1991 with permission by
Christian Literature Crusade
51 The Dean, Alresford, Hants SO24 9BJ and
Challenge Literature Fellowship
Revenue Buildings, Chapel Road, Worthing, W. Sussex BN11 1BQ.

CLC ISBN 0 900284 63 3
CLF ISBN 1 873496 00 1

Production and Printing in England for
Christian Literature Crusade/Challenge Literature Fellowship by
Nuprint Ltd, Station Road, Harpenden, Herts AL5 4SE.

CONTENTS

Introduction

God has written only one book—the Bible. Of the countless millions of books that have been written, it alone deserves to be called "the Book." The Bible offers eternal life to everyone who heeds its invitation, and spiritual food for Christians who want to grow. So it should be no surprise to us that this book continues to be the most read book in the history of the world. People of all lands and languages sense a strong attachment to it. What a priceless privilege and opportunity to read what God has written to us!

The Bible is a book for everyone. It is as open to the unschooled as it is to the Ph.D. at the university. Reading and studying the Bible is for all who approach it with reverence and desire. The Bible that lies on your desk or in your hand is a veritable invitation to blessing. It waits to be read and studied.

The sixty-six individual studies in *Simply Understanding the Bible* are designed to help you explore each book of the Bible in three stages. The first section of each study is entitled "Getting Started" and features the 🖙 symbol. The information associated with this symbol will be very helpful background information *before* you begin to read that particular book of the Bible.

Following the "Getting Started" material, you will see the "First Reading" symbol 🕮. This marks the material that you will find helpful *as you read* that book of the Bible. You will want to quickly scan this material before you read and then refer to it as often as necessary during your reading.

The division marked "Building Tools," designated by the 🗲 symbol, consists primarily of two groupings of information, "Important Passages" (or "Prominent Subjects"), and "Key Words." This material will hopefully provide tools for building a programme of personal Bible study. A study of key subjects or passages will help you in focusing your efforts. Likewise, doing a word study* can be very profitable—because it isolates ideas that were obviously important to the Bible author. Although there is much more to study in each book, we believe you will find ample treasure in the verses and passages highlighted in this section.

The Bible was meant to be read. An unread Bible is like refused food, an unopened love letter, a road map not studied, or a gold mine not worked. If you have put off reading your Bible, begin today to make reading and studying it a vital part of your life with God.

*All Bible quotations and key words are based on the New International Version of the Bible.

Why Read and Study the Old Testament?

The Old Testament is a thrilling and sobering book. Like the New Testament, it catapults us back in time. To a time when life was simpler, or was it? Paul tells us in the letter to the Romans, "For everything that was written in the past was written to teach us, so that through endurance and the encouragement of the Scriptures we might have hope" (15:4). He makes a direct link between life then and today. The struggles of the nation of Israel and individuals within it are *our* struggles too! The God of Abraham is the same God you talk to and seek to know. He has not changed.

What a joyous privilege to be able to read and study the lives of those who have sought to know God before us! There is much to learn about God himself through the insights of his *past* dealings with men. There are many compelling reasons why everyone should read and study the Old Testament. Here are a few:

1. The Bible is incomplete without the Old Testament. The life of Christ takes on its fullest meaning when seen against the backdrop of the prophecies about him in the Old Testament.
2. The ministry of Christ would be a mystery without the Old Testament. It is the Old Testament laws of a *holy* God that show why only the *sinless* Jesus could be the Saviour of all mankind.
3. The Old Testament gives God's perspective of world history in all centuries, showing him in absolute control, for ever.
4. The Old Testament is the setting of the New—spiritually, socially and historically.
5. Key doctrines of God and man are taught in the Old

Testament. These include who God *is* (i.e. holy, loving) and what he has *done* (e.g. creation, salvation). It is in the Old Testament that we secure an adequate reason why man is capable of benevolence (made in God's image) *and* of evil (depraved through the Fall).

6. The Old Testament is spiritual food for the believer. For example:

   a. Its laws and counsel show the way to please God (Exodus 20).
   b. Its Psalms encourage praise and prayer (see Psalm 107).
   c. Its testimonies inspire righteous living (Deuteronomy 31:24–32:47).
   d. Its accusations bring conviction of sin (Jeremiah 2).
   e. Its prophecies warn of danger and plant hope in the heart of all true believers (Zechariah 14).

7. In the Old Testament we learn the past, present, and future of God's chosen nation, Israel.

8. The Old Testament, along with the New Testament, is God's voice to us today. The New interprets the Old, and the Old Testament originates and illustrates the New.

Historical Setting of the Old Testament

All the books of the Old Testament are part of a historical chain. The first "link" in this chain is the Creation in Genesis 1 and the final link is the last prophecy of the closing book of the Old Testament, Malachi, about 430 B.C. The first eleven chapters of Genesis report highlights of the origin of man and the universe. In Genesis 12, the nation of Israel is "born" with God's call of Abram. The remainder of the Old Testament is a detailed description of God's dealings with this chosen nation.

The chart on the following page shows the period of Israel's history from its birth (around 2,000 B.C.) to about 400 B.C. Note on the chart this sequence of events in the life of the nation:

1. Bondage (2,000-1,500 B.C.)   cruel bondage in Egypt
2. Judges (1,500-1,000)   rulers of God's chosen nation
3. United kingdom (1,000-931)   the succession of kings Saul, David, and Solomon
4. Divided kingdom (931-586)   the North (Israel) vs. the South (Judah)
5. Captivities (722-536)   Israel in Assyria (722-536)
    Judah in Babylon (586-536)
6. Restoration (536-ff)   return to the land of Canaan

9

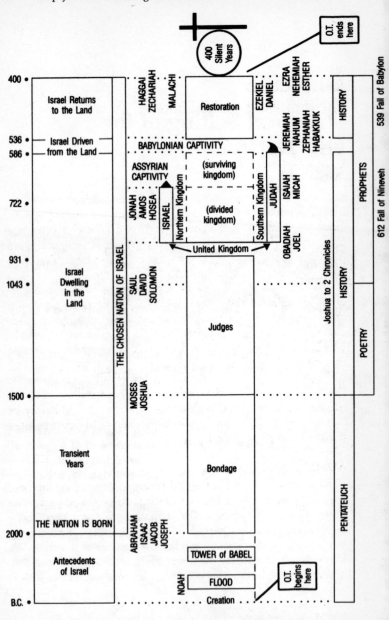

GENESIS
The Beginning of All Things

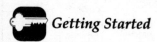 *Getting Started*

The book of Genesis rightly belongs at the beginning of the Bible, for it is a book about origins. It provides adequate answers to questions such as What? When? Who? and Where? in reference to God, man, and the universe. Its very first sentence gives powerful answers to such questions: "In the beginning God created the heavens and the earth."

God, the author of Genesis, has given the human race adequate information about the origin of the universe, the creation and fall of man, and the institution of a special nation, Israel. Also, continually throughout the book of Genesis, God reveals clearly who he is. We look for him in its pages and are not disappointed by what we find.

Accepting the Genesis account in its entirety as accurate is the key to believing and understanding the other sixty-five books in the Bible. Jesus spoke with certainty about the reliability of Genesis repeatedly.[1] Our perspective should be the same as his— it is the very Word of God.

AUTHOR AND DATE

The first five books of the Old Testament, including this one, are a unit called *the Law*. Moses has always been recognized as the divinely-inspired author of *the Law*, both by Old and New Testament writers alike.[2] There is no specified evidence for exactly when Genesis was written or where Moses was at the time. We know that God divinely inspired him to write about events that occurred when no one was yet alive (e.g., creation, etc.) as well as

---

[1] See Matthew 19:4 where Jesus clearly indicates that he considers Adam & Eve real, historical figures.
[2] Read Exodus 24:4 and Luke 24:44.

events that preceded him (e.g., Adam, Noah, etc.). But, for the God who spoke history into existence, such a feat is not difficult!

GEOGRAPHY

The locations described in the book of Genesis follow the progression of God's plan for mankind. Observe on the outline below the key places in which the narrative of Genesis occurs. You may want to consult the map on page 299 near the back of the book:

GARDEN OF EDEN ➡ BABYLON ➡ CANAAN ➡ EGYPT

PURPOSES

Among the main purposes of Genesis are to introduce God to the reader and document a reliable witness to the "beginnings" noted in the outline below. When reading and studying this book, we must keep in mind that the primary purpose of God was to introduce to us the "who" of the Bible. *He* is its central and essential figure.

THEME

In the beginning, God created everything, and his highest creation was the human race. Man sinned against God and reaped his judgment. God called Abraham to become the father of a righteous nation through whom he would bless all mankind.

KEY VERSE

"God saw all that he had made, and it was very good" (1:31a).

 First Reading

An excellent way to get a "feel" for the book of Genesis is to read the first verse of each chapter. Another way is to read the chapter or section titles included in some Bible translations. You will see the narrative moving from east to west and from all mankind down to a single family.

OUTLINE
The Beginning of All Things

The race as a whole 1:1–11:32
    A. Six days of creation 1:1–31 (Garden of Eden)
    B. Seventh day of rest 2:1–3
    C. Adam and Eve 2:4–25
    D. Fall of man 3:1–24 (Babylonia)
    E. First families 4:1–26
    F. Adam's descendants 5:1–32
    G. The Flood 6:1–9:29
    H. Birth of nations 10:1–11:32

Family of Abraham 12:1–50:26
    A. Abraham, father of Israel 12:1–25:18
    B. Isaac, child of promise 25:19–26:35 (Canaan)
    C. Jacob, transformed brother 27:1–37:2a (Egypt)
    D. Joseph, beloved son of Jacob 37:2b–50:26

OVERVIEW

The book of Genesis conveniently falls into two parts, chapters 1–11, which contain a history of the human race, and chapters 12–50, which detail the family of Abraham.

THE RACE AS A WHOLE				FAMILY OF ABRAHAM			
CREATION	FALL	FLOOD	BIRTH OF NATIONS	ABRAHAM	ISAAC	JACOB	JOSEPH
1	3	6	10	12	25:19	27	37:2b 50
EVENTS PROMINENT				PERSONS PROMINENT			
over 2,000 years				300 years			

•*The race as a whole* (chapters 1–11). This division rotates around four key *events*. Each section is actually a key passage of Scripture in its own right. As we read the texts, we should be attentive for personal spiritual applications. It is imperative that we seek to draw ourselves into the narrative of Genesis as we read.

• *The family of Abraham* (chapters 12–50). This division focuses on four *people*. Here we find the history of Israel during its first three hundred years, moving from Ur of Babylonia to Canaan, on into Egypt.

There is much to learn from the lives of those in the pages of Genesis, especially Abraham, Isaac, Jacob, and Joseph. It is by God's deliberate design that this division of Genesis is long!

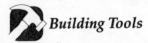 *Building Tools*

PROMINENT SUBJECTS

The book of Genesis is full of subjects deserving of deeper study and contemplation. Some of its richest treasures lie in the study of the *people* of Genesis, Cain, Noah, Abraham, Isaac, Jacob, and Joseph, just to mention a few. Pick one or two and follow their lives through Genesis. Be attentive for:

- Their most prominent failures and the consequences.
- The impact *their* lives had on their posterity.
- How they pleased God.

Another vast topic in Genesis is the character and nature of God. Below is a brief list of some of his attributes easily studied in Genesis. Write out what you see about his attributes in the passages indicated, how each attribute was manifested in the life of an Old Testament character, and what the attributes mean for you personally.

- God's power and wisdom—chapters 1–2
- God's love and mercy—chapters 3–4
- God's justice and holiness—chapters 6–9
- God's sovereignty—chapters 10–11
- God's salvation—chapters 12–25
- God's faithfulness—chapters 25–26
- God's grace—chapters 27–36
- God's providence—chapters 37–50

KEY WORDS

created, good, evil, curse, bless, great nation

EXODUS
Deliverance and Worship

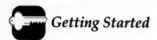 **Getting Started**

Joseph's last breath included these words, "I am about to die. But God will surely come to your aid and take you up out of this land to the land he promised on oath to Abraham, Isaac and Jacob" (Genesis 50:24). Joseph was referring to God's promise to his great-grandfather, Abraham.[3] When Joseph made that statement, the nation of Israel was few in number and living in the sunshine of Pharaoh's favour. Now, years later, the Jews have multiplied greatly and have become very strong.[4] Egypt's new king is fearful of the implications of a foreign "nation" living within a stone's throw of his throne! Suddenly, the children of Israel are viewed as a burden and threat by their Egyptian host. Pharaoh puts them to work as slaves of the kingdom. The book of Exodus opens with this scenario.

Exodus documents God's liberation of Israel from Egypt by means of signs, wonders, and a man named Moses. From Egypt the nation embarks on a journey to the land promised to Abraham, a land "flowing with milk and honey." The first half of the book details this deliverance; the second half is a record of the instructions given to Moses by God on how this new nation is to function.

AUTHOR AND DATE

Moses again claims authorship for this book.[5] We can assume that it was written soon after the completion of the Tent of Meeting (a portable tabernacle) around 1444 B.C. [6]

---

[3] Genesis 15:13,14
[4] see Exodus 1:7; 12:37; Numbers 1:46
[5] 17:14; 24:4; 34:27
[6] see 40:17

15

PURPOSE

Exodus stands as an eternal testimony to the *nature* of God (i.e., who he is), and the *works* of God (i.e., what he does). We can see God's attributes of holiness, power, justice, truth, mercy, and glory in the pages of this book. We also have repeated evidence of his faithfulness to his promises. The nature of God is evident in the Exodus account. But, in his deliverance of Israel from Egypt, we also can see "shadows" of themes developed further in the New Testament, such as forgiveness of sin, deliverance from sin's bondage, the preservation of his children, and what it means to walk with God.

THEME

God delivers the Israelites from bondage in Egypt and makes them his own "treasured possession" (19:5).

KEY VERSE

"And God said, 'I will be with you. And this will be the sign to you that it is I who have sent you: When you have brought the people out of Egypt, you will worship God on this mountain.'" (3:12).[7]

 First Reading

The chapter headings provide an excellent summary of the movements, people, and activities of the forty chapters of Exodus. Read them quickly in one sitting.

OUTLINE
Deliverance and Worship

> Deliverance   1:1–18:27
>   A. Bondage and oppression   1:1–11:10
>   B. Deliverance and provision   12:1–18:27
>
> Worship   19:1–40:38
>   A. Law   19:1–24:18
>   B. Tabernacle blueprint   25:1–31:18

---

[7] Exodus 12:51 is another key verse for this book.

C. Idolatry   32:1–34:28
D. Tabernacle construction   35:1–40:38

OVERVIEW

The book of Exodus deals with eight principal subjects:

- *Bondage*   1:8–22
- *Birth of Moses*   2:1–25
- *Call of Moses*   3:1–7:13
- *Ten plagues*   7:14–11:10
- *Passover*   12:1–51
- *The Red Sea*   13:1–15:21
- *Wilderness*   15:22–18:27
- *Sinai*   19:1–40:38
  * Law—chapters 19–24
  * Tabernacle blueprint—chapters 25–31
  * Idolatry—chapters 32–34
  * Tabernacle construction—chapters 35–40

Look at the survey chart below and seek to "locate" all the above subjects in the overall whole of Exodus, keeping in mind each subject's connection to the two main parts: Deliverance and Worship.

We can see God accomplishing his overall purposes of revealing who he is and what he does in the arrangement of the narrative material in Exodus.

DELIVERANCE		WORSHIP
1:1	12	19 40:38
BONDAGE AND OPPRESSION	DELIVERANCE AND PROVISION	LAW AND TABERNACLE
in Egypt	to Sinai	at Sinai

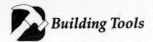 *Building Tools*

IMPORTANT PASSAGES

Below is a substantial list of topics that can be studied in the book of Exodus. As you read and contemplate their contents, seek to transfer the truths and concepts into your own life in the present.

• *Bondage* (1:8–22). How was their bondage similar to our bondage to sin? What did they *want*? What did they really *need*?

• *Moses' birth and "call"* (2:1–7:13). How can you see God answering the prayers of his people even when Moses is a child? What insights can you glean from these verses about prayer, God's call, or our limited perspective on the workings of God?

• *The plagues* (7:14–11:10). What areas of the Egyptians' lives were touched by each of the plagues?

• *Passover* (12:1–51). What was the significance of this celebration? How is our celebration of the Lord's Supper similar? What would it have been like to be there?

• *Red Sea deliverance* (13:1–15:21). Take some time to reflect on what *you* would have done if you had been an Israelite and why.

• *Wilderness journey* (15:22–18:27). What principles about God's provision can you dig out of these verses?

• *Ten Commandments* (20:1–17). Look at these again. Which ones give you the greatest struggle? Why?

• *The tabernacle* (25:1–31:18; 35:1–40:38). What influence would Egypt have had on the Israelites to demand that God would have to repeatedly stress his holiness? What influences are in our lives that could demand that we have a "tabernacle" to meet with God too? The idea of God living among the Jews was totally revolutionary.

KEY WORDS

"let my people go," redeem, command, covenant, altar, God's name. Tent (of meeting) appears repeatedly in chapters 26 and 40.

LEVITICUS
You Shall Be Holy for I Am Holy

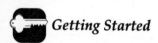 *Getting Started*

God wanted his beloved people, the Israelites, to enter into a covenant-keeping relationship with him. Leviticus is Israel's "book of worship." It answers the question, "How can sinful man fellowship with a holy God?" It is in the book of Leviticus that we are introduced to the concept of sacrificial atonement for sins through the elaborate system God established for approaching him. Through this book, Israel learns that sacrifice is the way to God.

The book's title[8] is derived from the name of the priestly tribe in Israel entrusted with the nation's ceremonial worship and care of their *place* of worship, the tabernacle—the tribe of Levi. God gave the contents of the book of Leviticus to Moses on Mount Sinai. Much more than a "religious" book, Leviticus contains regulations for the social life as well as the spiritual life of Israel.

Leviticus also contains the "shadows" of themes, doctrines and individuals that are fulfilled in the New Testament. The New Testament book of Hebrews sheds a great deal of light on the rituals and requirements of Leviticus. In fact, Hebrews is sometimes called "God's Commentary on Leviticus." From the book of Hebrews we learn that the Levitical priesthood and sacrifices were all intended to point the way to the "Lamb of God" and his once-for-all sacrifice for sin.

A brief comparison of the five books of the Law reveals the unique place Leviticus holds:

GENESIS	EXODUS	LEVITICUS	NUMBERS	DEUTERONOMY
ORIGINS of the nation	DELIVERANCE of the nation	LIFE of the nation	TEST of the nation	REMINDERS to the nation

[8] Leviticus means "that which relates to the Levites."

AUTHOR AND DATE

Moses wrote the book of Leviticus some time before the "wilderness wanderings" recorded in the book of Numbers, probably around 1440 B.C.[9]

PURPOSE

Leviticus is God's "manual" for his people explaining how sinful people can and must approach a holy God and live lives pleasing in his sight.

THEME

The inescapable theme of Leviticus is holiness: God is holy; therefore the people must approach him and serve him in holiness.

KEY VERSE

"I am the LORD who brought you up out of Egypt to be your God; therefore be holy, because I am holy" (11:45).

 First Reading

One way to scan Leviticus is to read its opening and closing verses (1:1–2 and 27:34) and the opening verse of each section of the outline below. From this quick reading, we immediately notice that Leviticus is primarily a book of laws and regulations.

OUTLINE
You Shall Be Holy for I Am Holy

The way to God   1:1–17:16
    A. Laws of offerings   1:1–7:38
    B. Laws of consecration of priests   8:1–10:20
    C. Laws of purity   11:1–15:33

---

[9] See Matthew 8:2-4; Leviticus 14:1-32 and Ezra 6:18 regarding evidence for Mosaic authorship.

The walk with God   18:1–27:34
    A. Holy people   18:1–20:27
    B. Holy priests   21:1–22:33
    C. Holy times   23:1–25:55
    D. Just recompense   26:1–46
    E. Holy vows   27:1–34

OVERVIEW

The book of Leviticus consists of two large sections, each devoted to a related theme: the way *to* God (chapters 1–17) and the walk *with* God (chapters 18–27). The Day of Atonement marks the centre of the book in content and theme. As you examine the chart below, notice how the idea of atonement really is the "centre" of the entire book:

WAY TO GOD				WALK WITH GOD			
LAWS:			DAY OF ATONE-MENT	HOLY:			
OFFER-INGS	PRIESTS	PURITY		PEOPLE	PRIESTS	TIMES	VOWS
1	8	11	16	18	21	23	26 27

• *The Offerings* (chapters 1–7). The way to God outlined in Leviticus was by means of sacrifices and offerings. The five main offerings of the Jews' worship are outlined here:

    (1) The burnt offering—voluntary; consecration to God (1:3–17; 6:8–13)
    (2) The meal offering—thanking God and offering lives for service (2:1–16; 6:14–23)
    (3) The peace offering—fellowship with God (3:1–17; 7:11–34)
    (4) The sin offering—forgiveness as sinners (4:1–5:13; 6:24–30)
    (5) The penalty offering—forgiveness for specific sins committed (5:14–6:7; 7:1–10)

• *The priesthood* (chapters 8–10). This section discusses the roles and responsibilities of those who served as mediators between man and God.

• *Purity* (chapters 11–15). This section contains a lengthy discussion of the various rules for hygiene and handling of disease, especially leprosy. Purity of body was important to God as well as purity of soul. God's intention was to "saturate" his people with the idea of holiness, a concept that was nearly erased from the corporate memory due to their exposure to the paganism of Egypt.

• *Day of Atonement* (chapters 16–17). This outlines the most important day in Israel's calendar. "It is the blood that makes atonement for one's life"(17:11b).

• *Holy people, places, and things* (chapters 18–27). In this large section, God outlines his requirements for holiness in a large number of areas and ways, from relationships to customs to feasts.

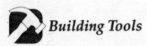 *Building Tools*

PROMINENT SUBJECTS

Leviticus would seem at first a distant and difficult book for modern Christians. But the themes that weave themselves through its pages are eternal and "profitable"[10] for us today. Using the "Key Words" section below, formulate an understanding of what Leviticus teaches about the subject of "man's sinfulness and God's holiness." (NOTE: Leviticus 18:1–5 is an excellent passage to study. Compare these verses to the holy conduct taught in the following New Testament verses: Ephesians 1:4; Colossians 1:21–23; 1 Timothy 2:8; Titus 1:8; 1 Peter 1:13–16; 1 John 1:6–7).

Also, what can be learned about God's desire to assume responsibility for making a way unto himself? What can you learn from Leviticus about the "Law"—its purpose and weaknesses?[11]

KEY WORDS

blood, life, holy, before the Lord

---

[10] see 2 Timothy 3:16–17
[11] Paul deals quite extensively with the failure of the Law in the book of Galatians; see especially Galatians 3:24.

NUMBERS
Journey to God's "Rest-Land"

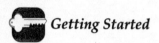 **Getting Started**

This book gets its name from two censuses (i.e., "numberings") of the people of Israel that occur in chapters 1 and 26. Numbers is God's record of the week and a half march from Mount Sinai to Kadesh Barnea in the plains of Moab opposite Jericho (see map, page 298), the rebellion that occurred there, nearly forty years of wandering through the desert, and the return to Kadesh where a *second* generation prepares to enter the rest-land God promised their parents. It chronicles a journey caused by unbelief and sin and shows us the seriousness of our choices. But, it also highlights the incredible faithfulness of God to keep his promises and to reward those who are obedient to him. It is a book rich in biographical insights, of both God and the men who loved him.

AUTHOR AND DATE

Moses wrote Numbers near the end of his life (early 1400s B.C.). He was probably camped with the people of Israel at Moab when he composed it.

PURPOSE

Numbers is the official record of the Israelites' journeys from Sinai to Moab. From its pages we learn of the cause and the cure for the forty years of wandering in the wilderness. It stands as one of the clearest and dearest illustrations of the faithfulness of God to his people and his promises.

THEME

Forty years of desert wanderings are God's judgment of disobedient and murmuring Jews, the original generation that fled from Egypt. Now with God's help a new generation of believers (the *children* of the first generation!) is ready to cross the Jordan into the promised rest-land of Canaan.

KEY VERSES

"We are setting out for the place about which the LORD said, 'I will give it to you.' ... Why is the LORD bringing us to this land only to let us fall by the sword?" (10:29; 14:3)

 First Reading

One way to scan the book of Numbers is to select key verses from selected "junctions" in the book. Read the verses listed below, keeping in mind the theme of Israel wandering in the wilderness:

VERSES	MAIN THOUGHTS
1:1	The Jews at Sinai, preparing to leave
1:1–3	The first census of the people is made
10:11	The journey to Moab begins
ch 13	Spies are sent out to look-over the promised land
14:1–25	The people (parents) murmur against Moses
22:1	The second generation arrives at Moab
26:1–4	A second census is taken
36:13	The people are across from Jericho, waiting to enter Canaan

OUTLINE
Journey to God's Rest-Land

Preparation for the journey (at Sinai)   1:1–10:10
    A. Inventory and assignments   1:1–4:49
    B. Final Instructions   5:1–10:10
The journey (to Moab)   10:11–21:35
    A. Sinai to Paran   10:11–12:16
    B. The spies' report   13:1–33
    C. The people's complaint   14:1–25
    D. God's judgment   14:26–45
    E. Desert wanderings   15:1–17:13
    F. Kadesh to Moab   18:1–21:35

At the gate to the land (at Moab)   22:1–36:13
    A. New problems   22:1–24:25
    B. Final preparations   25:1–30:16
    C. Concluding tasks   31:1–36:13

OVERVIEW

The entire book is one of movement. The nation is either moving toward Moab, wandering in the wilderness, or anticipating moving into Canaan. The chart below arranges the foregoing material into a graphic whole:

1:1 AT SINAI	10:11 TO MOAB	22:1 AT MOAB 36:13
Preparation for the Journey	The Journey	At the Gate to the Land
first census 1:1-3	spies – ch. 13 complaints – 14:1-25 punishments – 14:26-45	second across census from Jericho 26:1-4 36:13
few weeks	39 years	few months

• *At Sinai* (1:1–10:10). The first census of the people occurs and Moses arranges the tribes around with the Tabernacle in the center. Everyone, especially the Levites, are assigned tasks in preparation for the journey. The nation is confronted with needs for purification and dedication before they are allowed to depart. Finally, they depart for the Promised Land with the "pillar of cloud" as their guide.

• *To Moab* (10:11–21:35). The three million or so find the manna and Moses' leadership unsuitable and murmur to God about returning to Egypt. They reach Kadesh Barnea and "spies" are sent out to scout the land. The report of the majority creates another uprising, and finally God pronounces judgment—forty years of wandering. (NOTE: It is interesting to note that the Israelites accused God of bringing their children out into the wilderness to *die*. Because of their unbelief, God ends up taking their *children* into the Promised Land and *they* die in the wilderness!)

•*At Moab* (22:1–36:13). The second generation brings the nation "full circle." Another census is taken because nearly all the people from the first are now dead. Moses passes his leadership to Joshua and recounts the religious requirements to the nation. The book concludes with a description of the distribution of the Promised Land they are about to enter.

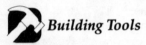

Building Tools

IMPORTANT PASSAGES

Below are some interesting subjects for further study from the book of Numbers:

(1) The debilitating effect of unbelief—Numbers 13:1–33 and Hebrews 3:12,18

(2) The contagious effect of negativism—Numbers 13–14

(3) Types of the Messiah in Numbers:

- the rock—Numbers 20:7–11 and 1 Corinthians 10:4
- the bronze serpent—Numbers 21:6–9 and John 3:14

(4) See if you can find seven times the Jews complained in chapters 11,13,16,20 and 21.

KEY WORDS

count, serve, desert, enemy, command

DEUTERONOMY
A Book of Remembrance

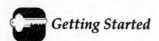 *Getting Started*

The title of this book literally means "second law." Forty years earlier, God delivered his Law to a nation that had just been delivered from bondage. They disobeyed in unbelief. Now, their children stand where they once stood, looking across the Jordan to the Promised Land. Moses delivers the *same* Law to them a "second" time. In fact, the bulk of the book consists of three sermons delivered by Moses to the Israelites. This time, regarding the Laws of God, Moses tells them, "They are not just idle words for you—they are your life" (32:47a).

As we would expect, the book is permeated with commands to obey God, the very thing their parents failed to do. Deuteronomy contains Moses' last words to the nation he had led for a generation. It is a sobering and serious book, and its pages contain truths as relevant for us as the morning news.

Because Numbers details "old" Israel under Moses' leadership and the book of Joshua records his administration over "new" Israel, the book of Deuteronomy serves as a sort of "bridge" between the two generations. Deuteronomy also contains our only account of Moses' death and burial, most likely recorded for us by his beloved successor and friend, Joshua.

AUTHOR AND DATE

Deuteronomy is Moses' last message to Israel around 1405 B.C., written in the desert east of the Jordan River (1:1).

PURPOSE

The book of Deuteronomy is one long plea for sincere obedience to God and his commands.

27

THEME

If you want to enter, claim and keep Canaan's "rest-land," remember your past (4:32), consider your present (5:33), and look to your future (28:2) through the eyes of obedience.

KEY VERSES

"And now, O Israel, what does the LORD your God ask of you but to fear the LORD your God, to walk in all his ways, to love him, to serve the LORD your God with all your heart and with all your soul, and to observe the LORD's commands and decrees that I am giving you today for your own good?" (10:12–13).

 First Reading

Reading the section titles for Deuteronomy in your Bible in one sitting will give you a good grasp of the "flow" of the book. You might also find reading the first verse of each chapter a good means to familiarize yourself with the book.

OUTLINE
A Book of Remembrance

    Introduction   1:1–5
    Remembrances of the past   1:6–4:43
    Commandments for the present   4:44–26:19
    Options affecting the future   27:1–30:20
    A change in leadership   31:1–34:12

OVERVIEW

Deuteronomy is built around three aspects of Israel's corporate life: their past, present, and future. The book itself falls into three sections, one devoted to each time span and its significance in the life of the nation.

Introduction	Remembrances of the PAST	Commandments for the PRESENT		Options affecting the FUTURE	CONCLUSION
	"Don't forget"	Ten Commandments ch. 5	Related Commandments	Blessings and Cursings	"Then Moses died"
1:1	1:6	4:44		27	31 34

•*Remembrances of the past* (1:6–4:43). In this section, Moses takes time to "review" the forty years they and their parents spent in the wilderness because of unbelief. His motive? To exhort them to faithful obedience by way of *reminder* (4:9).

•*Commandments for the present* (4:44–26:19). Moses lays out for them what God desires. The Ten Commandments are restated as well as a variety of other things God demands (5:32).

•*Options affecting the future* (chapters 27–30). Moses presents two options: Obey God and be blessed or disobey God and be cursed. The results of each are presented (28:2,15).

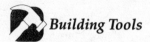 *Building Tools*

IMPORTANT PASSAGES

The book of Deuteronomy contains many rich chapters. Below are a few deserving of serious study. As you examine key phrases and words, contemplate the importance for *today*, the principles introduced almost three thousand years ago.

TOPIC	SCRIPTURES
The importance of learning from the past	chapters 1–4 (Note especially 4:9)
The importance of dependence upon God	chapter 8
The importance of the home	chapter 6
The example of a life well spent	chapters 31–34

KEY WORDS

remember (don't forget), obey, bless(ing), curse, covenant

JOSHUA
The Book of Conquest

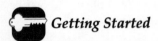 **Getting Started**

This book is named after its author, Joshua, the loyal and godly associate of Moses. It is the first of what are known as the "historical" books of the Old Testament. The five books of Moses, although also historical in nature,[12] are collectively called the "Pentateuch."

The book of Joshua chronicles a seven-year triumphant military campaign in Canaan under the valiant and brilliant leadership of Joshua in which the twelve tribes of Israel fight and defeat thirty-one armies! The idea that victory depends upon obedience to God looms large in this book.

Following the conquest, Joshua divides the land and the tribes settle in their assigned allotments. The book closes with the death of Joshua. It is interesting to note that unlike Moses, Joshua did not "groom" anyone to replace him as national leader.

AUTHOR AND DATE

Joshua, son of Nun, was born in Egypt of the tribe of Ephraim. He was one of the twelve selected to "spy" out Canaan when the Israelites first left Egypt. He and Caleb were the only ones from the scouting party that believed God would give them the land, just like he promised. Consequently, though the rest died in the wilderness, Joshua was allowed to enter the Promised Land.[13] He became Moses' successor, at the specific direction of God. The Bible also tells us that Joshua was indwelt by the Holy Spirit and filled with wisdom.[14] Joshua, whose name means "Jehovah is

---

[12] One can easily see that Genesis-Deuteronomy are historical accounts covering the time period from the origin of the universe to the creation of a new nation. There is also an obvious continuity from Numbers through Joshua that centres around the land of Canaan.

[13] see Numbers 13

[14] Numbers 27:15-23 and Deuteronomy 34:9

salvation," was totally committed to obeying and glorifying God. He stands as a model of faithful service for all time.

This book was most likely composed soon after the conquest of Canaan, around 1400 B.C.

PURPOSES

To reveal God's might, justice, mercy, and willingness to reward those who fear and obey him. Also, to document God's working through his servant, Joshua.

THEME

God is faithful to his promises. The land of Canaan, promised by God, was waiting to be occupied. Israel would have to *fight* to obtain what was promised. The obstacles they faced were part of God's plan to oust the idolatrous and corrupt nations from the land. Victory is secure if obedience is unconditional.

KEY VERSE

"So Joshua took the entire land, just as the LORD had directed Moses, and he gave it as an inheritance to Israel according to their tribal divisions. Then the land had rest from war" (11:23).

 First Reading

Look at each of the twenty-four chapters for a long enough time to identify key people and activities. We can also scan chapter or segment titles printed at the top or within the pages of our Bible.

OUTLINE
The Book of Conquest

Conquest of the land   1:1–12:24
    A. Preparation for war   1:1–5:12
    B. Conquest   5:13–12:24
Division of the land   13:1–21:45
Consecration for continued blessing   22:1–24:33
    A. Consecration of the Eastern tribes   22:1–34
    B. Consecration of the Western tribes   23:1–24:28
    C. Death and burial of Joshua and Eleazar   24:29–33

OVERVIEW

The book of Joshua consists of two main subject divisions, both focus on "the land." Chapters 1–12 deal with the *conquest* of the land, chapters 13–21 document the *division* of the land. The book concludes with three chapters chronicling the events surrounding the people consecrating themselves to God under a final charge from their soon-to-depart leader, Joshua. The chart below shows the two main divisions of the book:

CONQUEST OF THE LAND		DIVISION OF THE LAND	JOSHUA'S LAST DAYS
Preparation	Conquest	Allotments	Consecration
1	5:13	13:1	22:1 24

• *Preparation* (1:1–5:12). In this section, God gives his charge to Joshua and indicates to the people that Joshua has God's endorsement. They spy out Jericho, their first battle, and establish a "memorial" of stones as they cross the Jordan, the point of no return. This section concludes with the celebration of the Passover.

• *Conquest* (5:13–12:24). Joshua's strategy involved three campaigns: central (6–8), southern (9–10), and northern (11:1–15). His movements as a military leader are considered some of the best in history.

• *Land allotments* (13:1–21:45). This is the record of the joyous distribution of the land of Canaan. The promise to their forefather Abraham had finally been realized![15]

• *Consecration* (22:1–24:33). Like Moses before him, Joshua makes a final appeal to his people to "serve the Lord" in faithfulness and holiness. The book ends with a record of his death.

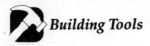 *Building Tools*

IMPORTANT PASSAGES

The overall lesson of the book of Joshua is the imperative of obedience to God, especially in the face of human difficulty. We

---

[15] see Genesis 12:7

would do well today to heed the example of Joshua and shun the examples of Israel's frequent acquiescence to self-determination.

Two of the choicest sections in the book for study are in its opening and closing chapters. The first chapter involves God's commission and encouragement to Joshua in 1:1–9. Read it slowly; study it carefully. What were Joshua's apparent needs? How did God seek to meet them? How do God's instructions to Joshua fit *your* life today? The book closes with Joshua's commission and encouragement to the people in 23:1–6 and 24:1–27. Note the words he uses. What does he say about households? What does this *mean*, in actuality? What does it mean for *you*, today? A third study you might find enriching is to compare the battle of the Christian on earth with that of Israel to enter Canaan.

KEY WORDS

land, war, battle, possess, obey

JUDGES
Great Leaders Rescue God's People

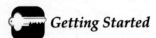 **Getting Started**

The book of Judges traces the history of Israel from the death of Joshua to the beginning of the monarchy, an unstable period of approximately 350 years. Judges is very different from the book of Joshua, however. While Joshua is primarily a record of the victory of God's people interspersed with defeat, Judges is a book of defeats punctuated by a few victories!

After the death of Joshua, God raised up leaders (called "judges") to rule the Israelites in peace and drive out enemies still residing in isolated pockets of Canaan. But, the people of Israel rejected God's help and wanted to be totally independent of his interference. This mentality is captured for us in a sobering statement from the pages of Judges, "In those days Israel had no king; *everyone did as he saw fit*" (21:25, emphasis added). God punished this national attitude by means of national defeat, and when the people finally repented of their sin, he forgave them and restored the land to peace. But, the fact that this "cycle of sin" repeated itself for thirteen different judges over 350 years makes us marvel at the loving patience of God! The chart on page 12 shows where this rather dark period of Israel's history fits. Also, it is during this time period that three famous Old Testament characters make their appearance: Deborah, the only female judge, Gideon, and Samson.

AUTHOR AND DATE

The reporter for the book of Judges is unnamed, although it is likely that Samuel, the main biblical character to follow, may have written it. The book was probably composed some time after the death of its last primary character, Samson, around 1051 B.C.

PURPOSE

Judges reports a repeated cycle of sin, judgment, repentance, and salvation. It chronicles the stormy relationship between the Israelites and their God. The book illustrates two glaring truths: (1) the desperate sickness of the human heart, and (2) God's long-suffering, patience, love, and mercy.

THEME

Sin grieves and angers God and carries within itself its own consequences. Repentance secures a loving and merciful response from God and a willingness to restore fellowship.

KEY VERSE

"But when the judge died, the people returned to ways even more corrupt than those of their fathers, following other gods and serving and worshiping them. They refused to give up their evil practices and stubborn ways" (2:19).

 First Reading

There are three primary divisions within Judges which you can scan quickly, looking for primary actions, people, and events:

- Background (1:1–3:6)
- Historical section (3:7–16:31)
- Appendix (17:1–21:25)

OUTLINE
Apostasies of God's People

Background   1:1–3:6
    A. Israel's failure   1:1–2:5
    B. God's dealings   2:6–3:6
History of the Judges (oppression and deliverance)   3:7–16:31
Double Appendix   17:1–21:25
    A. Idolatry of Dan   17:1–18:31
    B. Immorality of Benjamin   19:1–21:25

OVERVIEW

The survey chart below illustrates the three primary sections of Judges:

BACKGROUND	HISTORY OF THE JUDGES	DOUBLE APPENDIX
1:1	3:7	17:1 21:25
Principles of justice and mercy	Oppressions and deliverances	Further sin

• *Background* (1:1–3:6). These introductory pages summarize the Lord's dealings with his rebellious people and the demonstration of his principles of justice and mercy.

• *History of the Judges* (3:7–16:31). These fourteen chapters chronicle the essential events of the years of the thirteen judges.

• *Double appendix* (17:1–21:25). The book concludes with a depressing report of more moral and spiritual corruption within two tribes of Israel, a stark contrast from the conclusion to the book of Joshua.

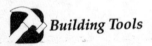 *Building Tools*

IMPORTANT PASSAGES

Below is a list of the thirteen judges of Israel. Look at each of their lives in the context of the mission God called them to. What were their strengths and weaknesses? How were they similar and different? How are the particular sin(s) they spoke out against manifested in *our* day?

- Othniel 3:7–11 (against the Mesopotamians)
- Ehud and Shamgar 3:12–31 (against the Moabites)
- Deborah with Barak 4:1–5:31 (against the Canaanites)
- Gideon, Tola and Jair 6:1–10:5 (against the Midianites)
- Jephthah, Ibzan, Elon and Abdon 10:6–12:15 (against the Ammonites)
- Samson 13:1–16:31 (against the Philistines)

It is also interesting to chart the cycle of sin as it reappears in the book of Judges. Use the Scripture references above and the five-fold list below and make a chart describing each of the cycles of sin:

(1) Rest—after victory come the blessings of rest.
(2) Rebellion—a new generation rebels against God.
(3) Judgment—God punishes them for their sin.
(4) Repentance—Israel repents and seeks God's forgiveness.
(5) Restoration—God raises up a judge to deliver the nation and bring them back into fellowship with him.

The life of Samson is also worth studying. Note especially how he compromised and its cost (13:1–16:31). What lessons can you learn from this judge?

KEY WORDS

"evil in the sight of the Lord," defeat, test, covenant

RUTH
The Story of a Woman From Moab

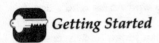 *Getting Started*

In the tumultuous years of the Judges, an era marked mainly by deceit, rebellion, and war, shines a woman of character, integrity, and consecration to God. Her name is Ruth. A Gentile, married to a Hebrew, she is one of the two women in all the Bible who has a book bearing her name![16]

Ruth is a Moabite widow who leaves her homeland to travel and reside with her widowed mother-in-law, Naomi. It is a story of devotion and faithfulness, pure love and loyalty, characteristics strangely absent from the pages of Judges. God's faithfulness is prominent too as he rewards Ruth with a godly husband, Boaz, the great-grandfather of King David![17] The Saviour of Israel, King Jesus, was to come from the line of David, which, at the time of Boaz, did not yet exist. We catch a glimpse of the majestic sovereignty and wisdom of God unfolding his plan of the ages.

AUTHOR AND DATE

We are unsure as to who wrote Ruth. The book may have been written some time during the reign of King David, 1011–971 B.C.

PURPOSE

The obvious purpose for the book of Ruth is to document a fragment of the marvelous way God brought forth the Messiah. We saw his wisdom operating in the preservation of the nation of Israel through Joseph in Egypt. Now we see how he orchestrated the continuation line of Judah, through which Jesus would come! Other attributes of God, such as his providence,

---

[16] The other is Esther.
[17] see 4:21-22

sovereignty, and grace, are also revealed in this short vignette.

We also have hints of what will become a dominant theme in the New Testament: God's plans to include the Gentiles in salvation's embrace. Ruth was a Gentile!

Boaz is also a "type" of Messiah, playing the role of redeemer to Ruth, a type of the church.

THEME

The grace of God extends to *all* who exercise faith. Ruth has become a worshipper of Israel's God, and the Lord brings her into a providential marriage with the man, Boaz. She bears a son, Obed, the father of Jesse, the father of King David, ancestor of Jesus, the Messiah of Israel.[18]

KEY VERSE

"But Ruth replied, 'Don't urge me to leave you or to turn back from you. Where you go I will go, and where you stay I will stay. Your people will be my people and your God my God'"(1:16).

 First Reading

Because of the brevity of the book, we can read it in one sitting easily. Look for "first impressions" of the main characters and the circumstances of their lives as you read. These names stand out: Naomi, Ruth, and Boaz.

The book ends with the word, "David." We see that in many ways, this book acts as a "bridge" between the era of the Judges and the monarchy, which will begin in the next book, 1 Samuel.

OUTLINE
The Story of a Woman From Moab

        A. To Moab and Return   1:1–22
        B. God's Gracious Provision   2:1–23
        C. A Claim to Kinship   3:1–18
        D. The Kinsman-Redeemer   4:1–17
        E. Conclusion   4:18–22

---

[18] see Matthew 1:5-6, 16

OVERVIEW

Use the chart below as you read, to assist you in your overall grasp of the book's themes and flow:

	chapter 1	2	3	4
NAOMI	Bereft of loved ones	Helping Ruth		Rejoicing over Obed
RUTH	Chooses to stay with Naomi	Seeks		Receives
BOAZ	_____	Sees	Loves	Marries

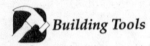

Building Tools

IMPORTANT PASSAGES

Study the life of Ruth from the dual aspects of life as *Ruth saw it* and life as *God directed it*:

(1) Ruth marries a Hebrew, a son of Naomi. He dies ten years later.
(2) Ruth and Naomi return to Bethlehem (1:6–22).
(3) Ruth meets Boaz, an Israelite, in Bethlehem (chapters 2–3).
(4) Boaz marries the widow Ruth (4:9–13a).
(5) Their offspring is the fountainhead from which will come the Messiah (4:13b–22; Matthew 1:1,5–6,16).

Another fruitful study lies in the role of "Kinsman-Redeemer" Boaz played in Ruth's life. As such, he typifies the same role that Jesus would one day play for all mankind. Compare the text of Ruth regarding Boaz's ministry to Ruth with the following New Testament passages regarding Jesus Christ: Romans 3:24; 1 Corinthians 6:20; Galatians 3:13.

KEY WORDS people, kinsman-redeemer, redeem

1 SAMUEL
Saul: The First King of Israel

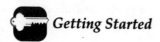

Getting Started

The book of 1 Samuel is a transitional book in the history of Israel, documenting the change in leadership from judges to kings. It begins where Judges left off, "In those days Israel had no king; everyone did as he saw fit" (Judges 21:25).

God had always desired to reign as King in the hearts and lives of his people. He wanted to govern them through leaders of *his* choice. But, eventually the people clamored for a king, so they could be like the ungodly nations around them. As the aging Samuel was approaching the end of his own life, they insisted he secure them a king, ". . . now appoint a king to lead us, such as all the other nations have" (8:5b). They rejected God's plan, and in so doing rejected *him* as their king! Only the Lord's unfathomable mercy spared the nation from being extinguished altogether.

The book of 1 Samuel centres on three dominant characters whose lives are inseparably intertwined: Samuel (Israel's last judge), Saul (the *nation's* choice for king) and David (*God's* choice for king). The book covers about sixty years of Israel's history, from the birth of Samuel to the death of Saul.

AUTHOR AND DATE

Like all the historical books of the Old Testament from Joshua to Esther, this book is anonymous. It is possible that Samuel was its author, writing between 1025–900 B.C.

PURPOSE

The book documents Samuel's "reform" of the spiritually and politically corrupt nation and its transition into a monarchy. King David is introduced as the epitome of a godly king and a foreshadow of Jesus Christ. The roles assumed by Samuel and

David of prophet, priest (intercessor), and king all point to their fulfillment in the one God-man, Jesus.

THEME

God is merciful and patient, always desiring to help his people. Although he commissions and calls men to shepherd and lead his people, they do not always remain faithful to his call.

KEY VERSES

"... from that day on the Spirit of the LORD came upon David in power.... Now the Spirit of the LORD had departed from Saul" (16:13b and 14a).

 First Reading

There are essentially three different ways we can scan the book of 1 Samuel: (1) reading the first verse of each chapter, (2) reading all the chapter or segment titles printed in our Bible, or (3) reading the opening and closing verses of each section shown in the outline below. Whichever method you choose, look for the three leading characters of the book: Samuel, Saul, and David.

SAMUEL

Samuel was the last judge of Israel[19] even though he and his mentor, Eli are not mentioned in the list of judges. Historically, the Jews have always esteemed Samuel as second only to Moses, as a man of God. The early chapters of this book are about the early years of Samuel.

SAUL

Saul was the first king of Israel, and as such occupies a primary position in chapters 9–31. The story of Saul's rise and demise is one of the saddest in all Scripture. He ends up losing the kingdom because of his obsession with pleasing people.[20]

DAVID

David was God's choice as a successor to Saul. He occupies

---

[19] see 7:6,15–17
[20] see 13:13–14 and 15:24

a central role in chapters 16–31, but his reign as king is actually the story of 2 Samuel. There we will see him as Israel's greatest and noblest king, but in 1 Samuel we see him waiting for a crown that Saul refuses to surrender to him. Saul becomes David's arch enemy, and the contrast of character recorded in 1 Samuel is stark indeed!

OUTLINE
Saul: The First King of Israel

        Samuel: The last judge   1:1–8:22
            A. Samuel's birth and call from God   1:1–4:1a
            B. The Ark of the Lord   4:1b–7:2
            C. Samuel the Judge   7:3–8:22
        Saul: The first king   9:1–15:35
            A. Saul the chosen king   9:1–12:25
            B. Saul the rejected king   13:1–15:35
        David: The great king   16:1–31:13
            A. David anointed by Samuel   16:1–17:58
            B. David attacked by Saul   18:1–21:9
            C. David in exile   21:10–28:2
        Saul's last days as king   28:3–31:13

OVERVIEW
Using the chart below, we can quickly see how intricately the lives of the three main characters are woven together in the book of 1 Samuel. Use the chart as you read and study:

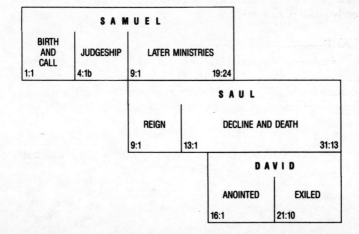

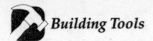

Building Tools

IMPORTANT PASSAGES

The book of 1 Samuel is virtually teeming with themes and ideas worth further investigation. Below is a partial list that will provide much insight for the faithful student of Scripture:

• *Samuel and Eli* (chapters 1–3). Examine their lives, especially the boy Samuel's sensitivity to God. What would *you* have done if you had been his mother? What about Eli's home? Did Samuel grow up in the "ideal" environment?

• *The ark of the Lord* (4:1b–7:2). What were the misuses and misconceptions about this piece of religious furniture? What was *God's* intention in the affair? What are modern equivalents for demanding God's "blessing" on our lives?

• *Obedience vs. sacrifice* (chapter 15). What was really wrong with Saul's conduct? Think this through. How are we like him? What pleases God and what doesn't, even though we might think it does?

• *David and Goliath* (chapter 17). What principles about spiritual warfare can you glean from this chapter? What truths about obeying God in the face of ridicule and ostracism?

KEY WORDS

pleased, ark, judge, king, Jonathan

2 SAMUEL
David: Israel's Greatest King

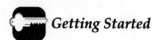 **Getting Started**

In the original Hebrew Bible, there was no division between 1 and 2 Samuel. They were one complete volume. Therefore, 2 Samuel should be viewed as the continuation of the themes and lives of those in 1 Samuel. In fact, the two books can be viewed as follows:

- Death of Saul—1 Samuel 31
- David's lament—2 Samuel 1
- David begins to rule—2 Samuel 2:1ff

David was the second king of Judah, crowned at thirty years of age and reigned for forty years.[21] His reign as king pivots around a single event in his life, an act of adultery with a woman named Bathsheba. His reign up to this point is marked by success and victory, but his personal life and that of the nation *after* the event is scarred with turmoil, civil war, and unrest.

In spite of his obvious failures as a leader and father, David is called a "man after God's own heart"[22] because of his penitent attitude and enduring devotion to God. A report of his career appears in three historical books[23] and many of the Psalms which he wrote. There are fifty-eight references to David in the New Testament alone. He is undoubtedly one of the key figures in the history of God's people.

AUTHOR AND DATE

The same person who penned 1 Samuel wrote the continuation of that story at the same time.

---

[21] see 2 Samuel 5:4–5; Saul (1043-1011 B.C.), David (1011-971 B.C.) and Solomon (971-931 B.C.)

[22] compare 1 Samuel 13:14 and Acts 13:22

[23] see 1 Samuel 16; 1 Kings 2:11; and 1 Chronicles 11-29

PURPOSE

God has preserved the account of 2 Samuel for two primary reasons:

(1) To record the highlights of the reign of Israel's greatest king around the topics of a king, a city, an agreement, and a kingdom.
(2) To teach crucial spiritual truths about the will of God, dependence on him, and sin and its consequences. Truths about walking with God abound in 2 Samuel.

THEME

When the Spirit of God is in control of a person's heart, blessing and success result. But when selfish desires are in control, it results in punishment and failure.

KEY VERSES

"And now, LORD God, keep forever the promise you have made concerning your servant and his house. Do as you promised, so that your name will be great forever. Then men will say, 'The LORD Almighty is God over Israel!' And the house of your servant David will be established before you" (7:25–26).

 First Reading

We can get a good feel for this book by reading the first verses of its main sections: 1:1,4; 2:1,4; 5:1–3; 11:1–4; 13:1; 21:1. We can also compare thirty-year-old David at the beginning of the book with seventy-year-old David at its close (1:1–4 and 24:24b–25).

OUTLINE
David: Israel's Greatest King

David's Reign   1:1–20:26
   A. Lament over Saul and Jonathan   1:1–27
   B. Reign over Judah   2:1–4:12
   C. Reign over all Israel   5:1–10:19
   D. David's sins   11:1–12:31
   E. David's troubles   13:1–20:26
Appendixes (various subjects)   21:1–24:25

OVERVIEW

The book of 2 Samuel records three phases of David's life: his TRIUMPHS, his SINS, and his TROUBLES. The chart below organizes the material around these three themes. Chapters 11 and 12 are the critical turning point for the king, for it is in these two chapters that we have the record of the series of sins he committed which would hunt and haunt him the rest of his days. In fact, the TROUBLES that constitute the bulk of the remaining chapters are God's judgments for those sins. Chapters 19 and 20 record David's welcome back as king after his own son had failed in an attempted military takeover. Unfortunately, his troubles continue on to the end of the book.

1	5	11	13	19	21	24
DAVID'S TRIUMPHS		DAVID'S SINS	DAVID'S TROUBLES			
REIGN OVER JUDAH	REIGN OVER ALL ISRAEL	SIN	PUNISHMENT	RESTORATION	APPENDIX	

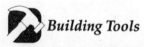

Building Tools

IMPORTANT PASSAGES

• *Death of a friend* (1:1–27). David's loss of his very best friend is documented here for us. Also, examine this man of God's response to the death of the man who wanted to kill him.

• *Death of a dream* (6:1–7:29). David returns the ark of God to its rightful place in Jerusalem and decides he wants to build a "house" for God. Instead, God tells David that he will build a "kingdom" for him! Spend some time thinking about what it was like for David to have this "dream" shattered. What can we learn from him?

• *Death of a conscience* (11:1–12:31). Study carefully what David did, why, and what he *didn't* do that he should have. What can *you* learn to protect yourself from sexual temptation and sin?

• *Death of a family* (13:1–20:26). Examine the "fruits" of David's adultery and murder within his own household.

KEY WORDS

sin, fight, kill, "before the Lord," Jerusalem

1 KINGS
A Kingdom Divided Against Itself

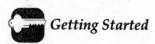 *Getting Started*

As the book of 1 Kings opens, David's reign is closing. He is an old man preparing to die.[24] His son, Solomon, is prepared to assume the reins of the kingdom. David's advice to his son is concise and simple:

(1) Be a benevolent but strong leader
(2) Obey God completely and explicitly
(3) If *you* obey God, he will fulfill his promise to *me*

Much of the book of 1 Kings is a dark record of Solomon's failure to heed his father's dying counsel. Although he succeeds in building a temple in Jerusalem as the *religious* centre for all of Israel, Solomon himself fails to make the Lord the centre of his *own* life. His own loyalties are divided between God and self, and the nation as a whole follows suit. By the time 1 Kings ends, the Jews are a divided nation with both portions sliding away from God.

The following diagram shows the major points of change in Israel's history during the ensuing years of the kings. The events of those years have four key milestones associated with them:

(1) The beginning of rule by kings (Saul, David, Solomon)
(2) The split of the kingdom into Israel (north) and Judah south)
(3) Israel taken captive by Assyria in 722 B.C.
(4) Judah taken captive by Babylon in 586 B.C.

---

[24] see 1:1 and 2:2

THE TWO KINGDOMS

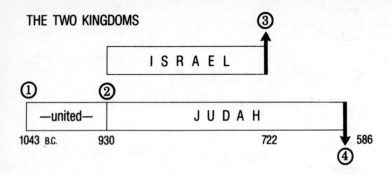

You will also find the charts on pages 288, 289, which list the kings of both kingdoms, very helpful as you read the books of 1 and 2 Kings.

AUTHOR AND DATE

One anonymous author wrote both 1 and 2 Kings. He was a Jewish captive in Babylon, like Jeremiah, probably writing between 562–536 B.C.

PURPOSE

To document in detail the welfare of the united kingdom under Solomon *and* the divided kingdom of Israel and Judah.

THEME

Solomon begins his rule over a united kingdom in glory and under the blessing of God promised to those who obey. After Solomon's death, enmities and jealousies rend the kingdom into rival factions. The internal troubles of God's people never cease from this point on.

KEY VERSES

"As for you, if you walk before me in integrity of heart and uprightness, as David your father did, and do all I command and observe my decrees and laws, I will establish your royal throne over Israel forever, as I promised David your father when I said, 'You shall never fail to have a man on the throne of Israel'" (9:4–5).

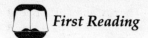

First Reading

Here is a scanning procedure that will be of assistance as you quickly peruse the pages of 1 Kings:

CHAPTERS	KEY CHARACTER/EVENTS
1–11	Solomon
12	Division of the kingdom
13–16	Rulerships of various kings
17–22	Elijah

OUTLINE
A Kingdom Divided Against Itself

United kingdom under Solomon   1:1–11:43
    A. Early years   1:1–4:34
    B. Building projects   5:1–9:9
    C. Last years   9:10–11:43
Divided kingdom: North (Jeroboam) and South (Rehoboam)
    12:1–16:34
Ministries of Elijah   17:1–22:53

OVERVIEW

As we read and study 1 Kings, it will help to keep the overview chart below in mind. The book falls into three main sections:

chapters 1-11	chapter 12	chapters 13-22
UNITED KINGDOM AT REST	SPLIT OF THE KINGDOM	2 KINGDOMS IN TURMOIL
God rules his people through a king: SOLOMON	↑ the pivotal chapter	God speaks to his people through a prophet: ELIJAH

• *The Reign of Solomon* (1:1–11:43). The rise and fall of one of Israel's greatest kings is documented. Note the splendor of David's dream, the temple, in chapters 5–9, particularly Solomon's prayer of dedication in 8:22–53. His later years of decline and demise are recorded for us in chapter 11.

• *The rending of the kingdom* (chapter 12). Petty rivalries and antagonisms erupt into secession from the kingdom. Solomon's son Rehoboam watches as his father's majestic kingdom of twelve tribes splits into two separate kingdoms with distinct kings. Ten tribes formed the northern kingdom of Israel and two southern tribes formed the kingdom of Judah. Jeroboam ruled the south and Rehoboam the north.

• *The ministry of Elijah* (16:29–19:21). The closing chapters of 1 Kings record the activities of one of Israel's most wicked kings, Ahab. The prophet Elijah plays a vital role in God's attempts to draw his people, via their king, back to himself. Elijah is one of the "greats" of the Old Testament.

 *Building Tools*

IMPORTANT PASSAGES

A number of exciting sections lie within the text of 1 Kings. Choose one or two and carefully examine them, paying special attention to what you can learn about God's character and what he requires of his children. Also, look for insights about what to do and not to do:

- Solomon's prayer of dedication   8:23–53
- God's warning and Solomon's demise   9–11
- Lessons about leadership   12:1–17
- Biography of a saint   17–19

KEY WORDS

David, father (his, my, your), obey, king, temple, riches (wealth), command, Elijah

2 KINGS
Kingdoms Taken Captive

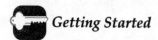 **Getting Started**

The book of 2 Kings continues the saga of 1 Kings. In fact, in the Hebrew Bible, the two books are one. The continuity is obvious when you compare the final three verses of 1 Kings and the opening two verses of 2 Kings. The book of 2 Kings concludes with the fall of the southern kingdom (see "The Two Kingdoms" on page 54).

Nineteen wicked rulers ascend the throne in Israel, all indifferent to the pleas and prophecies of God. Finally, they are taken into captivity by the ruthless Assyrians. Israel's "sister" to the south survives 150 years longer, but learns nothing from God's judgment on the northern kingdom and is conquered by the Babylonians and serves seventy years of captivity in Babylon.

Viewing the two books as a unit, some interesting facts emerge in comparing the beginning with the end:

- First Kings begins with a kingdom established in glory; 2 Kings ends with a kingdom dissolved in shame.
- First Kings begins with bright prospects for obedience; 2 Kings ends with tragic judgments for disobedience.
- First Kings begins with the dazzling splendor of the temple; 2 Kings ends with the smoke and flames of a temple in ruins.

AUTHOR AND DATE

Because 1 and 2 Kings are actually one work, the same person who wrote 1 Kings authored 2 Kings as well. The time of composition would be identical to that of 1 Kings.

PURPOSE

To complete the record of the kingdoms of Israel and Judah from the time of Ahab to the defeat and disintegration of the nations.

THEME

A nation that rejects God is rejected *by* God.

KEY VERSE

"So the LORD said, I will remove Judah also from my presence as I removed Israel, and I will reject Jerusalem, the city I chose, and this temple, about which I said, 'There shall my Name be'" (23:27).

 First Reading

There are twenty-five chapters in 2 Kings. As we turn the pages of our Bible and read the segment or chapter headings, we will observe the repeated mention of the names of the prophet Elisha and the kings of the northern kingdom (Israel) up to chapter 17. From then on, we see the names of the kings of the southern kingdom (Judah).

OUTLINE
Kingdoms Taken Captive

The divided kingdom: Israel and Judah   1:1–17:41
    A. Ministries of Elisha   1:1–8:15
    B. Kings of Israel and Judah   8:16–17:6
    C. Israel to captivity   17:7–41
The surviving kingdom: Judah   18:1–25:30
    A. Hezekiah to Zedekiah   18:1–23:30
    B. Judah to captivity   23:31–25:30

OVERVIEW

The survey chart below shows that 2 Kings has two primary focal points: a *divided* kingdom (1–17) and a *surviving* kingdom (18–25).

1	DIVIDED KINGDOM	18	SURVIVING KINGDOM	25
	Israel and Judah		Judah	
	MINISTRIES OF ELISHA		GOOD INFLUENCE OF KING HEZEKIAH	

ISRAEL TO EXILE   JUDAH TO EXILE

• *The ministry of Elisha* (1–13). From the fiery exit of his mentor Elijah, to his own death, Elisha stands as one of the most powerful of all Old Testament prophets.

• *The spiral toward judgment* (14–17). Following Elisha's death, the northern kingdom accelerates its corruption to the point where God's judgment falls and the nation is dispersed.

• *A bright spot for Judah* (18–21). The reign of king Hezekiah is one of the few truly hopeful seasons in the corporate life of God's people. But the brightness fades when his successor, his son Manasseh, turns Judah away from God.

• *One final attempt for reform* (22–25). Josiah, the last righteous king of Judah makes an attempt to reform the nation. He succeeds in changing their behaviour but not their hearts. The book ends with Jerusalem destroyed and the people taken captive.

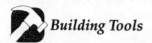 *Building Tools*

IMPORTANT PASSAGES

The contrast of character within the pages of 2 Kings is staggering. Examine the lives of the people listed below. List as many righteous qualities and deeds as you can for each godly person and as many unrighteous qualities and deeds as you can for the ungodly.

"THE GOOD GUYS"	Scripture	"THE BAD GUYS"	Scripture
Elisha	3–13	Jehu	9–10
Joash	11–12	Athaliah	11
Hezekiah	18–20	Manasseh	21
Josiah	22–23		

KEY WORDS "the eyes of the Lord," sins, evil, removed

1 CHRONICLES
Highlights of David's Reign

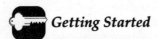 *Getting Started*

The two books of Chronicles are a *sacred* history of the Jews covering the same time period as 1, 2 Samuel and 1, 2 Kings, with an introduction that contains an abbreviated discussion of Israel's ancestry to Adam. The distinction these books hold is that they "chronicle" the *spiritual* life of the nation more than merely the political intrigue and treachery that characterized most of the narratives in Samuel and Kings, and they only report the details concerning the southern kingdom, Judah.

The books focus especially on the southern kingdom of Judah in general and the line of David in particular, covering the period of Jewish history from the reign of David to the Babylonian captivity. The books stress the critical value of pure worship of the one true God of Israel. In terms of examples, David's life shines brighter than any other in Israel's history when it comes to worship. The very existence of the Psalms, much less their content, testify to this truth.

Chronicles was written for the exiled Jews in Babylon, now preparing to return to their homeland.[25]

AUTHOR AND DATE

The author of these two books is unknown. There is a possibility that they were penned by the scribe Ezra, between 450–425 B.C.

PURPOSE

The two books of the Chronicles are an assurance to those in captivity that God is still interested in them and loves them. The message of the books is that he will restore and forgive those who

---

[25] read 2 Chronicles 36:22-23

repent of their sins and worship him in faithfulness and truth. The books give much attention to the temple as the focal point for worship.

THEME

God can restore his wandering people.

KEY VERSE

"Yours, O LORD, is the greatness and the power and the glory and the majesty and the splendor, for everything in heaven and earth is yours. Yours, O LORD, is the kingdom; you are exalted as head over all" (29:11).

 First Reading

When we scan the first nine chapters, we are immediately struck with a *multitude* of names—the descendants of Adam. This is clearly a genealogical history. From chapter 10 to the end of the book, *one* name dominates the narrative—David. This last section is a biographical history.

OUTLINE
Highlights of David's Reign

> Genealogies   1:1–9:44
>   A. Of Adam to the restoration   1:1–9:44
> The Reign of David   10:1–29:30
>   A. Background: the death of Saul   10:1–14
>   B. David's rise to the throne   11:1–20:8
>   C. David's latter days   21:1–29:30

OVERVIEW

The historical material in 1 Chronicles is arranged in a very specific and unique fashion. The chart below helps us see how the author constructed the book:

THE ANCIENT WORLD		DAVID	
ANCESTORS		HISTORY	
FORE-FATHERS	NATIONS	DAVID'S RISE	DAVID'S FINAL YEARS
1	2	10	21 29

• *Ancestors* (chapters 1–9). The author records the family lines of God's chosen people, descended from Abraham (1:27–28), and destined ultimately to be the line through whom the Messiah would come. He divides this material into a genealogy of the forefathers and a longer section of the nations that arose from them.

• *History* (chapters 10–29). This section reports the highlights of the life of the nation's greatest king, David. It chronicles his establishment of Jerusalem as the focal point around which the rest of the nation's history will revolve and David's attempts to make sure that the kingdom is following God with its whole heart after his death.

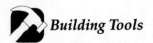 *Building Tools*

IMPORTANT PASSAGES

First Chronicles records three prayers of David that are rich in worship and deserve closer attention. As you study them, look especially for insights regarding David's understanding of God's character and his own attitudes of worship and thanksgiving. What can you learn? Where should you change?

• A psalm—16:7–36
• A prayer—17:16–27
• A prayer—29:10–20

KEY WORDS

David, sons, priests, praise

2 CHRONICLES
The Descendants of David

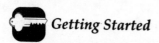 **Getting Started**

Whereas David was the central figure of 1 Chronicles, his descendants occupy centre stage in 2 Chronicles. This book carries the reader through four centuries of Judah's history: from the time of David's son, Solomon, to the end of the exile in Babylon. The narrative begins in splendor around the throne of Solomon and ends in disaster with the city and its temple destroyed.

The spiritual health of Judah can easily be charted through the book of 2 Chronicles. The reader will see an immediate connection between the spiritual life of the leader and the spiritual health of the people. Second Chronicles is rich in lessons on leadership and its effects.

AUTHOR AND DATE

The same as 1 Chronicles.

PURPOSES

The book of 2 Chronicles serves as an illustration and a warning that God's long-suffering and mercy have limits. God repeatedly warned the southern kingdom to repent, but they failed to listen, thinking that God would never destroy his own "home" (i.e., the temple). The Lord shows us in this book that *he*, not his house, is to be the focal point of his people.

THEME

God honours and blesses those who honour him but judges those who forsake and reject him.

KEY VERSE

"Solomon son of David established himself firmly over his

kingdom, for the LORD his God was with him and made him exceedingly great" (1:1).

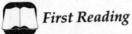 *First Reading*

An excellent way to secure an overall sense of this book is to quickly read three short sections that spotlight pivotal events in the narrative:

1:1; 9:29–31	Solomon, the third king of the united kingdom
10:16–19; 11:5–17	The united kingdom splits into north and south
36:11–23	The southern kingdom is taken into captivity

OUTLINE
The Descendants of David

The reign of Solomon   1:1–9:31
    A. Wisdom and wealth   1:1–17
    B. The temple   2:1–7:22
    C. Other achievements and his death   8:1–9:31
The kingdom of Judah   10:1–36:23
    A. Division of the kingdom   10:1–11:23
    B. The kings of Judah   12:1–36:16
    C. The exile of Judah   36:17–21
Epilogue: Plans for restoration   36:22–23

OVERVIEW
Before you begin to read 2 Chronicles, you will find it helpful to review the overview sections of 1 and 2 Kings. The following chart provides a graphic presentation of the narrative of 2 Chronicles:

1	10	12	36:15-23
KING SOLOMON	SPLIT	KINGS OF JUDAH	FALL
UNITED KINGDOM	OF THE	SOUTHERN KINGDOM	OF THE
	KINGDOM		KINGDOM

• *The united kingdom* (chapters 1–9). This section deals with the reign of David's son, Solomon. Its primary focus is on the temple that he constructed as his father instructed.

• *The divided kingdom* (chapters 10–11). The split of the nation due to the folly of Solomon's young son is documented. Two kingdoms result, each with its own king.

• *The southern kingdom* (chapters 12–36). The remainder of the book records the rise and fall of Judah's spiritual health. One conclusion is inescapable from these chapters: the leadership of any people determines its spiritual condition. See the list of kings for the two kingdoms on pages 288, 289. The book ends with a message of hope: a proclamation from Cyrus, king of Persia, allowing the Jews to return to Jerusalem!

 *Building Tools*

IMPORTANT PASSAGES

Two themes weave themselves through the fabric of 2 Chronicles: prayer and reformation. Below are some suggested sections that contain good study material on these two themes. As you read, look for principles and applications for today.

Prayer
- What circumstances prompted the prayer?
- What was the outcome of prayer?
- Who prayed?
- Passages: chapters 11,13–15,17,20,26–27,30–32,34

Reformation
- What was the moral dilemma?
- Who was the "man of God" that brought reform?
- What was the ultimate outcome? (i.e., did it last?)
- Passages: chapter 15; 17:6–10; 23:16–19; chapters 29–31; chapters 34–35

KEY WORDS

"Lord . . . God," chosen, temple, Babylon

EZRA
Restoration and Reform

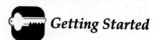 **Getting Started**

The prophet Jeremiah had predicted the Babylonian Captivity,[26] God's just judgment upon Judah for her sin. But he had also prophesied a return to the land from which God's people were driven,[27] evidence of his mercy and grace. When we read the closing verses of 2 Chronicles and the opening verses of Ezra, we see that Ezra continues the story of Chronicles, but we also see the beginning of the fulfilment of Jeremiah's prediction: The Israelites will return to Jerusalem.

You will find the chart about Old Testament history on page 12, and the map, "Israel, Judah and Surrounding Lands," on page 299 helpful as you read and study the book of Ezra. Ezra is the story of the return of the exiles to Jerusalem. A preliminary group of nearly fifty thousand return with Zerubbabel to begin the arduous and painful task of rebuilding the temple. It takes them nearly twenty-five years to complete the job! After more than half a century, Ezra leads the second major group of Jews (most of them priests) back home. Just as Zerubbabel sought to restore the physical foundations of the nation, Ezra seeks to rebuild the spiritual fibre of God's people. The book of Ezra covers each of these two migrations.

AUTHOR AND DATE

Ezra may have written this book soon after returning to Jerusalem from Babylon, around 450 B.C.[28] Hebrew tradition tells us that he served in Babylon as a high priest, that he originated the

---

[26] see Jeremiah 25:11–12
[27] see Jeremiah 29:10,12
[28] see Ezra 7:8–9

Jewish synagogue form of worship,[29] and collected the Old Testament books into a unit. Ezra's main contribution has to do with the preservation of the Law of God and its importance in the everyday lives of his people.

PURPOSE

This book is an excellent documentation of God's fulfilment of his promises of restoration through the prophets Isaiah and Jeremiah.[30]

THEME

God is faithful to his promises.

KEY VERSE

"Now these are the people of the province who came up from the captivity of the exiles, whom Nebuchadnezzar king of Babylon had taken captive to Babylon (they returned to Jerusalem and Judah, each to his own town)" (2:1).

 First Reading

This is a short book of only ten chapters, but its mood is positive and uplifting because of the underlying theme of God's blessing. You will notice, in perusing its pages, a unique feature: the inclusion of various separate letters.[31]

Glancing quickly at chapter and segment titles, we notice that the returning Jews had many important tasks to perform and problems to face.

---

[29] There is no real mention of when synagogues appeared as a legitimate form and place of Jewish worship. We can assume that they began some time during the time frame of Ezra because they did not exist *before* the Exile, yet when the New Testament opens, they are literally everywhere in the known world.

[30] see Isaiah 44:28 and Jeremiah 29:10-14

[31] note: 1:2-4; 4:6-23; 5:8–17 and 7:11-28

OUTLINE
Restoration and Reform

Restoration under the governor: Zerubbabel   1:1–6:22
    A. The journey   1:1–2:70
    B. The task: Rebuilding the temple   3:1–6:22
Reforms under the priest: Ezra   7:1–10:44
    A. The journey   7:1–8:32
    B. The task: Dissolving mixed marriages
      8:33–10:44

OVERVIEW

The ten chapters fall fairly evenly into two divisions, with chapter 7 beginning the second section. The chart below will help you see how the book is constructed. It is devoted to the ministries of two faithful servants of God: Zerubbabel and Ezra.

FIRST RETURN OF EXILES	THE WORK	SECOND RETURN OF EXILES	THE WORK	
1	3	7	8:33	10:44
RESTORATION UNDER ZERUBBABEL		REFORMS UNDER EZRA		

• *Restoration under Zerubbabel* (chapters 1–6). This section deals with the difficult task of rebuilding the temple. Tears flow freely as the people realize what they've lost through disobedience. Progress is hindered on every side. The determination of Zerubbabel to be faithful to his assignment from God shines magnificently.

• *Reformation under Ezra* (chapters 7–10). After much prayerful preparation, Ezra and a much smaller group begin the four-month trek to their homeland. Ezra arrives to discover that although the temple is standing, the people are not! Spiritual pollution and cleansing characterize these final chapters.

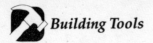

Building Tools

IMPORTANT PASSAGES

An interesting study lies in comparing the two distinct ministries recorded in this book. Make a list of the verbs that are associated with Zerubbabel and Ezra. Notice the different trials and blessing each experienced. Obedience to God was the cause.

Another fruitful study is found in the penetrating prayer of penance in chapter 9. As you read Ezra's prayer, look for his association with the problem rather than separating himself from it (e.g., his use of "us," "we," "our," rather than "they," "them," etc.). What is your perspective on the problems in your church, or of Christianity in the nation? Have you ever found yourself as troubled over your own sins against God? Do you pray with the passion of Ezra, asking for righteousness and holiness to be established in your life and those around you?

KEY WORDS

return, Jerusalem, order(s), temple, law

NEHEMIAH
Building for Security

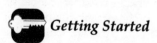 *Getting Started*

The book of Nehemiah begins its story twelve years after the narrative of Ezra closes. Nehemiah, cupbearer to the Persian king, Artaxerxes, led a small third expedition to Jerusalem to assist his brethren in the task of rebuilding the walls of the city. In biblical times, a city without walls was an open invitation to marauding thieves and enemies.

Nehemiah's experience is very similar to that of Zerubbabel and Ezra before him. Local opposition retards progress on the project, but eventually through unusual dedication and effort, the zealous band completes the walls in fifty-two days. Their enemies, realizing that there had been divine assistance, admit in shame that God himself was Nehemiah's helper.[32]

The remainder of the book records Nehemiah's attempts to ''rebuild'' the moral fibre of the city's occupants – which in many ways proves to be a more difficult task!

AUTHOR AND DATE

The book is named after its chief character and author. It opens with a clear statement of authorship, "The words of Nehemiah son of Hacaliah" (1:1). This book was written around the time the walls were reconstructed, 420 B.C.

PURPOSE

The book continues the theme of Ezra, namely preserving the truth of God's enduring faithfulness to his promises to his people.

---

[32] 6:16

THEME

God can restore the damage done by sin.

KEY VERSE

"Then I said to them, 'You see the trouble we are in: Jerusalem lies in ruins, and its gates have been burned with fire. Come, let us rebuild the wall of Jerusalem, and we will no longer be in disgrace'" (2:17).

 First Reading

Nehemiah is a relatively easy book to read because it is an action-packed narrative of only thirteen chapters. Reading the opening verses of each chapter will provide us with an immediate feel for the book.

OUTLINE
Building for Security

> The work   1:1–7:73a
>> A. Planned   1:1–3:32
>> B. Threatened   4:1–6:14
>> C. Finished   6:15–7:73a
> The worship   7:73b–13:31
>> A. Revival   7:73b–10:39
>> B. Redistribution   11:1–12:26
>> C. Rededication   12:27–43
>> D. Reform   12:44–13:31

OVERVIEW

The survey chart below shows the two major divisions of the book of Nehemiah: The *work* and the *worship*. The chapters describing the work are mainly about *material* tasks, and the worship chapters reveal the *spiritual* ministries God wanted his servants to perform for the people.

THE WORK		THE WORSHIP	
1	7:73b		13:31
Leadership by a man		Revival of a nation	
Rebuilding the wall		Obeying the law	

• *The work* (chapters 1:1–7:73a). This section begins with Nehemiah receiving permission to return to his homeland to assist in the wall project. Upon arriving in Jerusalem, Nehemiah faces various difficulties regarding his assignment. The section closes with the completion of the walls.

• *The worship* (7:73b–13:31). After the walls were completed and the people once more had physical security, Nehemiah turned his attention to the need for spiritual purity. Ezra taught the people from the Scriptures, repentance and revival occurred, and a renewed sense of commitment emerged.[33]

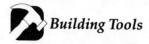 *Building Tools*

IMPORTANT PASSAGES

Nehemiah also contains a great number of references to prayer. It is obvious that prayer is an essential ingredient when seeking to be faithful to the clear commands of God. Following is a short list of verses from the book that deal with prayer. Read them slowly and thoughtfully, gleaning all you can about prayer: 1:4–11; 2:4; 4:4–5,9; 5:19; 6:9,14; 13:14,22,29,31.

Another excellent section in Nehemiah contains the building projects. Read chapters 1–7, paying close attention to all you can learn about walking in holiness in the midst of the realities of the world of work. Take notes. What can you apply to your own work or home environment.

KEY WORDS

pray, work, wall, rebuild, remember

---

[33] see 8:1ff; 9:1-38; 10:29ff

ESTHER
A Story of Providential Care

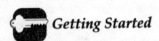 **Getting Started**

The book of Esther is one of the least known books of the Bible, yet it records a vital piece of Old Testament history. We can recall from our reading of Ezra and Nehemiah that there were three pilgrimages from captivity to Jerusalem. What these accounts do *not* reveal, however, is that a large time period elapsed between the first two, and had it not been for Esther, the second and third expeditions would never have become realities! In fact, the entire Jewish nation might have vanished like the dark at sunrise, had it not been for this little known heroine.

Esther was a devout Jewish orphan maiden who lived in Shushan, Persia's principal city. She was nurtured by her cousin, Mordecai, who was an official in the palace of King Xerxes.[34] After the king had divorced his wife, he conducted an unusual "beauty parade" to select a new wife. His choice? Esther. This made her the queen over an enormous empire.[35]

Our study of Esther will reveal God's providence in preserving his people so he could fulfil the promises he had made regarding their return to the promised land.

AUTHOR AND DATE

Although Esther is the main character of the book, it is unlikely that she was the author. Perhaps Ezra or Nehemiah wrote this parenthetical account some time around 483-473 B.C.

---

[34] Xerxes is the Persian name for the king. The Hebrew name for the same king is Ahasuerus.
[35] We learn from 1:1 that Xerxes ruled over 127 provinces from India to Ethiopia. Some have estimated that 2 to 3 million Jews were living in Babylonia and Persia during this time, not to mention the Gentile population.

PURPOSE

The major purpose of the book of Esther is to show how a host of Jews living in exile were spared by means of a Gentile king from a well-planned extermination.

THEME

The fate of all nations—good or bad—is in the sovereign hands of God.

KEY VERSE

"For if you remain silent at this time, relief and deliverance for the Jews will arise from another place, but you and your father's family will perish. And who knows but that you have come to royal position for such a time as this?" (4:14).

 First Reading

Because the book is a continuous story, it is best to read it at one sitting, if possible. The book opens and closes with the theme of respect and honour. It begins with the exaltation of Xerxes, the Persian king, for his greatness, and ends with Mordecai receiving honor from his fellow Jews for saving the nation.

OUTLINE
A Story of Providential Care

The Jews are threatened   1:1–3:15
    A. The setting   1:1–2:23
    B. The plot   3:1–15
The Jews are spared   4:1–10:3
    A. Deliverance   4:1—9:16
    B. Commemoration   9:17–32
    C. Exaltation   10:1–3

OVERVIEW

The book of Esther consists of two main sections: the *Threat* to the Jews, and the *Deliverance* of the Jews. Refer to the following survey chart as you read and study Esther.

THE JEWS ARE THREATENED			THE JEWS ARE SPARED		
Gentile setting	Elevation of a Jewess	Threat against the Jews	Influences of a Jewess	Deliverance of the Jews	Exaltation of a Jew
1	2	3	4	8	10:1 10:3

• *Gentile setting* (chapter 1). King Xerxes asks his queen Vashti to entertain the guests at his party. When she refuses, he banishes her from the kingdom and begins to search for a new queen.

• *Elevation of a Jewess* (chapter 2). Esther, an orphaned Jew, raised by her cousin Mordecai, wins the "beauty contest" Xerxes conducts and is chosen to be queen. Mordecai discovers a plot against the king and informs the new queen, who promptly warns Xerxes and saves his life. Morcecai is honoured in the sight of all.

• *Threat against the Jews* (chapter 3). One of the king's men, Haman, rises in power and is infuriated when Mordecai will not bow down to him. As a result, Haman devises a plan to exterminate all the Jews from the kingdom. Mordecai informs Esther of his plot and asks her to tell the king.

• *Influence of a Jewess* (chapters 4–7). Through prayer and fasting, Esther carefully reveals her Jewish heritage and Haman's plot to the king. Angered, Xerxes demands that Haman be hanged on the very gallows he had built for Mordecai.

• *Deliverance of the Jews* (chapters 8–9). Xerxes orders everyone in the empire to recognize the Jews' place and power. The Jews are spared slaughter! The king helps establish the Feast of Purim as a perpetual reminder of God's great deliverance.

• *Exaltation of a Jew* (chapter 10). The book concludes with Mordecai being exalted to the right hand position of the king and being highly respected by his fellow Jews.

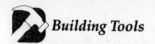 *Building Tools*

IMPORTANT PASSAGES

The providential care of God permeates this exciting story. This is especially important when we realize that the name of God does not appear even once in the narrative! Make a list in the spaces below, and chart the evidence that God was indeed the Master Controller behind the entire story:

Chapter/Verse	Evidence of God's Providence

Another fruitful study is to contrast the character of Haman with that of Mordecai. Find as many ways as possible where they are different. Pay close attention to the outcome of each of their lives, both short term and ultimate.

KEY WORDS

Jew(s), banquet, kill

JOB
Knowing God Better Through Adversity

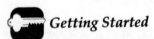 **Getting Started**

Job was a native of the land of Uz, northeast of Palestine. The opening comments of the book give us a valuable preliminary glimpse into his character: "In the land of Uz there lived a man whose name was Job. This man was blameless and upright; he feared God and shunned evil . . . He was the greatest man among all the people of the East" (1:1,3b). Although we have very little chronological data in Scripture to pinpoint *when* he lived, it is likely that Job lived shortly before the call of Abraham.[36] If so, the nation of Israel did not yet exist, even in promise.

The book opens in heaven with a conversation between God and Satan in which the Devil accuses Job of honouring God only because he has such a comfortable life. The Lord allows Satan the opportunity to prove his slander by giving him permission to remove Job's circle of comfort through loss of his possessions, family, reputation, and finally his health. Three of Job's friends hear of his calamity and come to "comfort" him. Their "comfort" consists of trying to get Job to admit that his misfortune was a consequence of his own sin.

The book concludes with a powerful appearance of God himself in which he vindicates Job and causes him to recognize that he is sovereign and can be trusted for who he is, even in the face of perplexing or seemingly contradictory circumstances.

AUTHOR AND DATE

The human author of this book is anonymous and the date of composition is also unknown.

---

[36] Genesis 12:9

PURPOSE

God's primary purpose is to reveal valuable and powerful insights about his own character. God's sovereignty, love, and wisdom shine through this account. By giving the reader an advantage that Job himself never had, namely access to the first two chapters of the book in which we discover the *cause* of Job's calamity, God provides some insight to the question of why righteous people suffer.

THEME

Trust in God is based on confidence in his character ("who") rather than an explanation for my circumstances ("why").

KEY VERSE

"But he knows the way that I take; when he has tested me, I will come forth as gold" (23:10).

 First Reading

An excellent way to approach this rather lengthy book is to read the opening and closing sections and scan the intervening chapters. Read chapters 1–2, "Job is Tested;" chapter 3, "Job Despairs;" and chapters 38–42, "God Speaks to Job." Then, go back and scan the chapter headings or segment titles for chapters 4–37.

OUTLINE
Knowing God Better Through Adversity

Prologue: Job is tested   1:1–2:13
Dialogue: The drama unfolds   3:1–37:24
   A. Job despairs   3:1–26
   B. Job is counselled   4:1–37:24
      1. by his three friends   4:1–31:40
      2. by Elihu   32:1–37:24
Epilogue: Job is approved by God   38:1–42:17

OVERVIEW

The survey chart below shows that a few opening chapters tell how Job's trials began as a result of the accusations of Satan against Job. Job's life is dismembered by the Accuser of the Brethren[37] until Job cries out in anguish that he regrets being born. The bulk of the book is a record of the feeble and faulty attempts of Job's friends to explain his pain to him. The book concludes with God himself addressing Job regarding his life, whereupon Job repents in humility in the face of God and is restored to health and success.

JOB IS TESTED	JOB DESPAIRS	JOB IS COUNSELLED	JOB IS APPROVED	
1:1	3:1	4:1	38:1	42:17
Challenge of Satan	Complaint of Job	Judgments of man	Voice of God	
Problem of pain		Men's wrong and deficient answers	God's perfect answer	

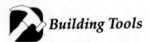

Building Tools

IMPORTANT PASSAGES

Two important subjects for the Christian dominate the book of Job:

(1) Our personal enemy, Satan
(2) The problem of suffering

What can you learn about Satan's desires and designs for the children of God from the *first* two chapters of this book? Be thorough as you ponder his statements to God, his intentions and actions toward Job, and the degree of "liberty" he has in our lives.

What can you learn about the problem of pain and suffering

---

[37] This account of Satan's conversation with God regarding Job provides us with invaluable insight into the title ascribed to Satan in Revelation 12:10: the one who "accuses the brethren" before God.

from the *last* four chapters of the book? How does understanding who God is provide adequate (though not exhaustive) answers? If you have additional time, examine the wrong answers to the problem of suffering offered by the four "counsellors" who exhausted Job with their shallow wisdom.

KEY WORDS

curse, cry, crush, wicked, upright, wisdom, why?

PSALMS
The Songbook of Israel

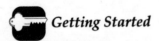 **Getting Started**

The Psalms constitutes the longest and possibly most often-quoted book in the Old Testament. It is primarily a collection of 150 hymns of worship and praise. Our word, "Psalms," actually comes from a Greek word that has the meaning, "music on string instruments."[38] When the individual psalms were first brought together as one hymn book in the pre-Christian era, the Hebrew title assigned it was *Tehillim*, meaning "praise songs." This worship motif reaches a climax at each of the conclusions of the five major divisions within the Psalms with a benediction or doxology of praise. The chart below shows the five divisions within the Psalms, their respective themes and doxologies:[39]

PSALMS	GROUP 1 1	GROUP 2 42	GROUP 3 73	GROUP 4 90	GROUP 5 107 150
DOXOLOGY AT	41:13	72:18,19	89:52	106:48	150:6
WORSHIP THEME	ADORING	WONDERING	CEASELESS	SUBMISSIVE	PERFECTED

AUTHOR AND DATE

At least seven individuals contributed to the book of Psalms, David furnishing the largest number.[40] Most of the psalms were written between 1000–900 B.C., with a few exceptions.[41]

---

[38] *Unger's Bible Dictionary*, Chicago: Moody Press, 1966. Page 898.

[39] The worship themes used here are taken from G. Campbell Morgan.

[40] Seventy-three psalms bear his name and he perhaps wrote some of the fifty others that are anonymous.

[41] Psalm 90 is credited to Moses and Psalm 126 is from the post-exilic period.

PURPOSE

There are many obvious purposes for such a book. The major purpose, however, is to reveal God and the way to worship and walk with him. Prominent in the Psalms are the person of God, the Son of God, the Word of God, the works of God, and the people of God.

The Psalms are intended by design and content to inspire, challenge, comfort, and transform everyone who encounters them. The spirit of this book should be the very breath of anyone who calls himself a true believer.

THEME

God is worthy of our adoration and praise.

KEY VERSE

"Let everything that has breath praise the LORD. Praise the LORD" (150:6).

 First Reading

The book is too long to scan like you would any other. However, there are some things you can do to get a "feel" for it. Reading the doxology that concludes each section (see chart above) is an excellent way to draw yourself into a sense of praise. Another quick way to familiarize yourself with the book is to scan the "titles" assigned each psalm. A third way is to read the opening verse of each psalm. As you scan the book you will also notice that the psalms differ greatly in length (e.g., Psalm 119 is 176 verses long and Psalm 123 is only four verses long).

OUTLINE

The book of Psalms has no real "outline" other than the loose thematic arrangement shown in the above chart.

OVERVIEW

(See chart, on preceding page.)

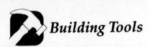 *Building Tools*

IMPORTANT PASSAGES

Two ways to study the psalms are to examine them one-by-one or by "type." Whichever method you decide to use will depend upon your interest and time. Below is a listing of psalms arranged according to types. As you study the psalms, do so in a spirit of worship and expectant praise. (You may discover that praying the very words of the psalm *back to God* can be one of the most worshipful experiences one can have in Bible study.) Also, jot down words or phrases that recur, noting the verses surrounding them. Finally, try to give each psalm you study a "title" based on what you feel is the dominant thought or idea it captures.

THE PSALMS ARRANGED BY TYPE

PSALM TYPE	EXAMPLES
Teaching/instruction	1,5,7,15,17,50,73,94,101
History of Israel	78,105–106,136
Hallelujah	106,111–113,115–117, 135,146–150
Confession	6,32,38,51,102,130,143
Intercession	86
Thanksgiving	16,18
Messianic[42]	2,20–24,41,68,118
Nature (God's handiwork)	8,19,29,33,65,104

KEY WORDS

Following is a list of words that appear repeatedly enough in Psalms to be considered "key words." Their occurrences are too numerous to list. Be attentive for them as you read and study: praise, worship, pray, thanksgiving, (thy) word, trust, happy, wicked, hope, fear, save, refuge.

---

[42]These psalms predict the comings of Christ; either his *first* coming in humiliation or his *second* coming in glory.

PROVERBS
Walking in the Fear of the Lord

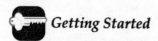 *Getting Started*

While David was a composer of worship songs, his son Solomon was a writer and compiler of proverbs. David composed to help us worship God; Solomon wrote to help us walk among mankind.

The word "proverb" has a root meaning of "to be like." The word "like" appears repeatedly in Proverbs (e.g., "*Like* a muddied spring or a polluted well is a righteous man who gives way to the wicked" [25:26]).

We are told from Scripture that Solomon penned over three thousand proverbs in his life. The book of Proverbs contains only about one-third of them. Yet, the wisdom contained within its pages crosses all cultures and eras and provides us with more than enough to think about and do in a lifetime!

AUTHOR AND DATE

Practically the entire book of Proverbs was written by Solomon some time between 950-900 B.C.[43]

PURPOSE

Solomon's primary purpose is stated as the book opens, "for attaining wisdom and discipline; for understanding words of insight; for acquiring a disciplined and prudent life, doing what is right and just and fair" (1:2–3). Wisdom is sometimes called knowledge in action or seeing life from God's point of view. Both are apt descriptions of what Solomon had in mind when he wrote Proverbs.

---

[43]The first verses of Proverbs 30 and 31 indicate different authors for these two chapters.

THEME

True wisdom is built upon an acknowledgement of God for who he is.

KEY VERSE

"The fear of the LORD is the beginning of wisdom, and knowledge of the Holy One is understanding" (9:10).

COMPARISON TO JOB AND PSALMS

Now that we have already studied Job and Psalms, here is how these two books compare with Proverbs:

BOOKS	KEYNOTES	USES
JOB	Questionings and reasonings	Answers from God and man
PSALMS	Worship	Handbook of devotion
PROVERBS	Observation and reflection	Guide to practical living

 First Reading

Reading the first verse of each chapter of Proverbs is a simple yet effective way to scan the book.

OUTLINE
Walking in the Fear of the Lord

Who is a truly wise man?   1:1–9:18
How does a wise man live?   10:1–22:16
An Appeal to action   22:17–24:34
A description of godliness   25:1–29:27
Epilogue: The sayings of Agur and Lemuel   30:1–31:31

OVERVIEW

The survey chart below shows the major organizational distinctions for the book of Proverbs:

PROVERBS

Introduction	FOUNDATION OF WISDOM 1		APPLICATIONS 10			31
	Especially for youth 1:7	8:1	— For all —			
	"My child"	"Wisdom"	"But"	"And" 16	Exhortations, comparisons and descriptions 22:17	

Looking at the chart above, you will notice that:

(1) The first nine chapters present wisdom as the foundation of life. The remaining chapters apply those truths to daily living.

(2) The first seven chapters are addressed especially to youth. (Notice "Listen my son . . . " of 1:8, the opening words of this section.)

(3) Wisdom is the keynote of chapters 8 and 9. As you read these chapters, notice how often the words "wise" and "wisdom" appear.

(4) Chapters 10–22 are short, one-verse maxims that often hinge on the words "but" or "and."

(5) The remaining chapters, 22:17–31:31, are a compilation of wise sayings, comparisons, and descriptions.

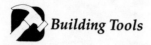

Building Tools

IMPORTANT PASSAGES

There are few books in the Bible as saturated with biblical riches as Proverbs. One can scarcely read a line without facing some practical implication from the truth it holds. The apostle James said that if we can control our *tongue*, we can control our entire being.[44] Study the subject of your speech through the book of Proverbs. Be prepared for God to speak!

[44]James 3:2

Another excellent topic to follow through Proverbs is that of daily conduct. Record all the insights you discover about getting along with others.

KEY WORDS

The following is a list of words that appear repeatedly enough in Proverbs to be considered "key words." Their occurrences are too plentiful to list. Pick one or two and keep a record of where they occur and in what context: wisdom, knowledge, understanding, fool, foolish, fear of God, life, but, commands, right, evil, my son, like.

ECCLESIASTES
Vanity Under the Sun, but Hope Is in God

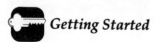 **Getting Started**

Ecclesiastes is the fourth of the poetical books in our English Bible: Job, Psalms, Proverbs, Ecclesiastes, and Song of Solomon. It is the second of three written by Solomon, "son of David, king in Jerusalem" (1:1). The title, Ecclesiastes, is a Greek word that translates the Hebrew, *koheleth* which means "preacher" or "teacher." This is the word "Teacher" in the book's opening verse.

Some have called the book of Ecclesiastes the "journal" of a desperate man. Its author records a seemingly endless list of pursuits, pleasures, and pondering of a life lived apart from God. The book is very depressing yet brutally honest about trying to enjoy life without consideration for the Author of life.

Ecclesiastes concludes with a powerful section about life's meaning and purpose being inseparable with an obedient and loving relationship with God. It stands today as the clearest and most sobering warning in all of Scripture for those who would seek to "do their own thing."

AUTHOR AND DATE

Though not specifically named, Solomon is commonly recognized as the author of Ecclesiastes. Because of the extensive list of personal experiences outlined in it, he probably penned this book during his later years, around 900 B.C.

PURPOSE

Ecclesiastes shows how futile and useless it is to pursue materialistic, selfish, earthly goals as ends in themselves. The book points to God as the only source of lasting personal fulfilment and meaning.

THEME

Life is meaningless apart from God, the Author of life.

KEY VERSES:

"'Meaningless! Meaningless!' says the Teacher. 'Everything is meaningless!'... Now all has been heard; here is the conclusion of the matter: Fear God and keep his commandments, for this is the whole duty of man" (12:8,13).

 First Reading

An excellent way to get a feel for the book is to read the introductory verses (1:1–11) and the concluding verses (12:8–14). How Solomon arrives at his conclusion after the depressing introduction is contained in the intervening chapters. Reading the first verse of each chapter will give us a few hints in the meantime.

OUTLINE

Vanity Under the Sun, but Hope Is in God

Introduction: All is meaningless   1:1–11
First sermon: Purpose with God   1:12–3:15
Second sermon: Worship of God   3:16–5:20
Third sermon: Gift from God   6:1–8:13
Fourth sermon: Knowledge of God   8:14–12:7
Conclusion: Fear God   12:8–14

OVERVIEW

The survey chart on the following page lays the book out. Solomon begins with the dilemma of life's apparent futility, "everything is meaningless"(1:1). In the text that follows, four sermons are presented in which Solomon recounts his quest for hope and happiness. All along his journey was the constant reminder of his opening statement.

By the time he ends his journal, his conclusion is brief yet profound: "Here is the conclusion of the matter: Fear God and keep his commandments, for this is the whole duty of man" (12:13). The wisest man on earth records his folly and return to true wisdom in the book of Ecclesiastes.

ECCLESIASTES

Introduction	Observations, conclusions, and counsel	Conclusion
1:1	1:12	12:8 12:14
"All things are useless."	SERMONS	"Honour God."
1:2	① 1:12 ② 3:16 ③ 6:1 ④ 8:14	12:13

• *Reading the sermons* —The four sermons are numbered on the survey chart above. As you read each sermon, notice the opening references to the meaninglessness and futility of life. Then look for glimmers of hope in the verses that follow. This pattern of gloom and hope is repeated in the sermons.

 *Building Tools*

IMPORTANT PASSAGES

A number of prominent themes are distributed throughout the book of Ecclesiastes. Chief among them is the idea of the utter meaninglessness of life "under the sun." Following is a listing of the references to life's futility. Examine them and jot down any insights, thoughts, or further questions that result from your study, especially in regard to the *specific areas of one's life* Solomon is addressing: 2:15–26; 4:4–16; 5:10; 6:6–9; 7:4; 8:10,14.

KEY WORDS

God (the creator), wisdom (wise), know (knowledge), work, "under the sun," "chasing the wind"

SONG OF SOLOMON
A Love Song

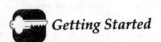 *Getting Started*

The Bible tells us that Solomon wrote over a thousand songs in his lifetime.[45] But, by his own admission, he calls *this* the "song of songs."[46] This is his magnum opus of songs. It has also been called "The Song of Songs." It is a human love story, set in a quaint countryside motif. The main characters are a Shulamite woman, a man, and the friends of the woman. It is a wonderfully poetic representation of the joys and heartaches of conjugal love.

But the book is more than merely a human love story. It is also an illustration of the love between the Lord God and his people, even though his name appears nowhere in the text. This spiritual relationship of love between God and man is explained further in the New Testament book of Ephesians, which teaches the intimate relationship between Christ (Bridegroom) and his Bride (the church).[47]

The Song of Solomon has always been highly regarded by Jews for its spiritual application and insight. Portions of it have been sung on the eighth day of Passover, the first and greatest of the Jews' annual religious feasts.

AUTHOR AND DATE

Solomon is the author by his own statement. He probably wrote this particular song while he was still quite young and had not yet been drawn away from his pure devotion to the Lord by his seven hundred wives.[48]

---

[45] see 1 Kings 4:32
[46] Song of Solomon 1:1
[47] Ephesians 5:25-32
[48] see 1 Kings 11:3-4

APPROACHING THE BOOK

The love described within the pages of the Song of Solomon is pure, wholesome, and glorifying to God. Beyond that, however, it portrays the beautiful spiritual relationship between Christ and those whom he has redeemed. As we prepare to read the words of the lover, the highest and ultimate application we should seek to make is that this is *Jesus our Savior speaking to us*, his beloved ones.

PURPOSE

The Song of Solomon accomplishes two primary purposes. First, it extolls the beauty, honor, and purity of human love within the context of marriage. Second, it illustrates the majesty and intimacy of *Christ's* love for each member of his body, the church, and illustrates what *our* response to that love should be.

THEME

I belong to the one who loves me, and I should love him in return.

KEY VERSE

"My lover is mine and I am his" (2:16a).

 First Reading

The book consists mainly of a series of dialogues between a lover (Solomon) and his beloved. Most editions of the Bible identify who the speakers are at the beginning of each new paragraph. Use these helpful distinctions as you read the book.

OUTLINE
A Love Song

> Title   1:1
> Courtship days   1:2–3:5
> Wedding   3:6–5:1
> Married life   5:2–8:14

A. Troubled dream of separation   5:2–6:3
B. Mutual love of husband and wife   6:4–8:4
C. The seal of their love   8:5–14

OVERVIEW

At 3:11 we see a reference to King Solomon's wedding day. This is one reason for titling the earlier chapters, "Courtship Days," and the succeeding chapters, "Married Life." Now, read the book again, using this pivot in the material as a guide.

SONG OF SOLOMON

LOVE FIRST EXPRESSED AND EXPERIENCED		LOVE TRIED AND TRIUMPHANT
COURTSHIP DAYS	WEDDING	MARRIED LIFE
1	3:6	5:2 8:14

 *Building Tools*

IMPORTANT CONCEPTS

Life with Christ and in Christ has a deep and satisfying joy for the Christian right now, today. And the joys of this sweet communion are a foretaste of the glories yet to come when the Lord returns to claim his Bride. Study the Song of Solomon with an eye toward an allegorical interpretation of the book. How is the "lover" like Jesus, and how is the "beloved" like us?

KEY WORDS

love, lover, lovely, beautiful, come

THE WRITING PROPHETS

Sixteen prophets wrote the seventeen books of prophecy in our English Bible. In addition to their prophecies in written form, these men also had a wide range of ministry through speaking at public gatherings in the temple or in the streets. For future generations of God's people, us in particular, their major work was in the form of written prophecies.

Whereas the priests spoke to God on behalf of man, prophets spoke to man on behalf of God. Their two-fold task was to *forthtell* and *foretell*. Forthtelling centred around the repeated phrase, "Thus says the Lord..." It involved teaching, warning, exhorting, and comforting. Foretelling involved the prediction of future events involving nations (especially Israel) and the Messiah.

The chart on the following page shows the three main periods during which they ministered and wrote (a more comprehensive listing with specific dates for each prophet, as well as the times associated with Ezra, Nehemiah and Esther is on page 290). Also, a chart comparing the four major prophets is on page 291.

THREE PERIODS OF THE PROPHETS

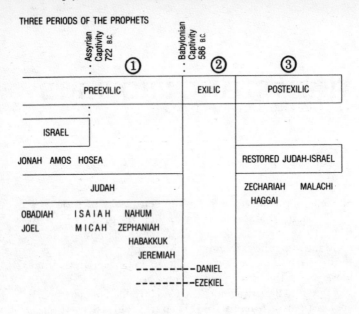

- *Preexilic prophets*—Eleven prophets ministered during the years leading up to the Assyrian Captivity of the northern kingdom (722 B.C.) and the Babylonian Captivity of the southern kingdom (586 B.C.). Notice the two big clusters of four prophets each:

1. To Assyrian captivity: *Amos* and *Hosea*, prophets primarily to Israel; *Isaiah* and *Micah*, prophets mainly to Judah.
2. To Babylonian captivity: *Nahum, Zephaniah, Jeremiah*, and *Habakkuk* (all to Judah).
3. Three earlier prophets: *Jonah* (Israel), *Obadiah*, and *Joel* (both to Judah).

- *Exilic prophets* —Two of the four major prophets were prophets during the Babylonian Exile: *Daniel* and *Ezekiel*.
- *Postexilic prophets* —The three prophets who ministered after the Babylonian Exile were *Zechariah, Haggai*, and *Malachi*. The first two served in the early years of Israel's return to the land, and *Malachi* ministered at the close of this period of restoration. He was the final voice from God until John the Baptist.

ISAIAH
The Glorious Throne of the Lord

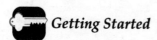 **Getting Started**

In our Bible, the book of Isaiah leads the list of the seventeen prophetical books. The authors of the first five of these are called the "Major Prophets"[49] because of the relative *length*, not importance, of their prophecy. Isaiah is the most-quoted Old Testament prophet in the New Testament, and also contains the largest number of prophecies surrounding the Messiah, Jesus.

The man Isaiah was not the first of God's prophets. He was a divine messenger to the southern kingdom of Judah (1:1) during the tumultuous period when the northern kingdom of Israel was taken captive to Assyria.[50] A detailed report of the historical setting of Isaiah's prophetic ministry can be found in 2 Kings 14–20.

AUTHOR AND DATE

The book opens with a claim to authorship and date, "The vision concerning Judah and Jerusalem that *Isaiah son of Amoz* saw during the reigns of Uzziah, Jotham, Ahaz and Hezekiah, kings of Judah" (1:1). The time frame in which these kings ruled was 740–690 B.C. The name "Isaiah" means "salvation is of Jehovah," a theme that virtually permeates the second half of this prophecy.

PURPOSE

The prophecy of Isaiah has three primary purposes, two of which were immediate and the third which was more future-oriented:

---

[49] The "Major Prophets" include: Isaiah, Jeremiah, Lamentations, Ezekiel and Daniel.
[50] see 2 Kings 17:16-19; also the chart, "Three Periods of the Prophets" on page 92.

(1) To speak out against the sin of the people and the impending judgments of God (chapters 1–39).
(2) To foretell Judah's captivity by an enemy from the east, the Babylonians (39:6–7).
(3) To predict the first and second comings of the Messiah (chapters 40–66) and other events surrounding the end times (e.g., 65:17).

THEME

The God of Israel is a holy yet compassionate God.

KEY VERSE

"And they were calling to one another: 'Holy, holy, holy is the LORD Almighty; the whole earth is full of his glory'" (6:3).

 First Reading

Isaiah is a long book of sixty-six chapters, so a couple of brief scannings at first will help us from getting lost in the book's many details. Reading the first verse of each chapter is one good way of first scanning. A second aide is to read the verses associated with the three main ideas in the book, namely:

- The opening of the book—1:1
- The change of theme—40:1–2
- The conclusion of the book—66:22–24

OUTLINE
The Glorious Throne of the Lord

Judgment of the Lord   1:1–39:8
    A. Prophecies to Judah   1:1–12:6
    B. Prophecies to foreign nations   13:1–23:18
    C. Warnings and promises   24:1–35:10
    D. History   36:1–39:8
Comfort of the Lord   40:1–66:24
    A. Salvation promised: The one true God
        40:1–48:22
    B. Salvation provided: The Messiah   49:1–57:21
    C. Salvation realized: God on his throne   58:1–66:24

OVERVIEW

The survey chart below divides Isaiah's message into two parts: *Judgment* (chapters 1–39) and *Comfort* (chapters 40–66). A good memory aid for the divisions of Isaiah is that the first thirty-nine chapters remind us of the thirty-nine Old Testament books, and the twenty-seven remaining chapters remind us of the message of grace and redemption found in the twenty-seven New Testament books. We can see why Isaiah has been called "The Miniature Bible!"

JUDGMENT OF GOD (39 chapters)	COMFORT OF GOD (27 chapters)
1	40 66
Holiness, righteousness, and justice of God	Grace, compassion, and glory of God

The Judgment of God

• *Prophecies to Judah*—(1:1–12:6). God's people have turned against him, so terrible times are coming for them.

• *Foreign prophecies*—(13:1–23:18). One example: "Her time is at hand and her days will not be prolonged" (13:22, speaking of Babylon).

• *Warnings and promises*—(24:1–35:10). Messages of hope and promise if the people will return to the Lord.

• *History*—(36:1–39:8). These chapters review the reign of King Hezekiah who ruled over Judah during Isaiah's day.

The Comfort of God

These twenty-seven chapters are wonderful, bright messages within the book. Comfort is the prevailing note in the three groups of nine chapters each:

• *Group One* (chapters 40–48). Consists of comparisons between the true God of Israel with the false gods of their neighbours.

• *Group Two* (chapters 49–57). Centres on the coming Messiah, especially his role as the "Suffering Servant."

• *Group Three* (chapters 58–66). This final group describes the final restoration of God's people and ends with God on the throne, receiving the respect of all people.

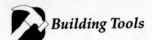 *Building Tools*

IMPORTANT PASSAGES

- *Songs* (chapters 5,12,35,54)
- *Judgments on Judah* (chapters 1–12)
- *Isaiah's commission as a prophet* (chapter 6)
- *Six "woes"* (chapters 28–33)
- *Book of comfort (the Coming of Christ)* (chapters 40–66)
- *Suffering and glories of the Messiah* (52:13-53:12)
- *The end times* (chapters 58–66)

KEY WORDS

Following is a list of words that appear repeatedly enough in Isaiah to be considered "key words." Because of the length of the book, the occurrences are not listed. Pick one or two and underline them in your Bible as you read. Then go back and arrange them and summarize what Isaiah has to say on these topics: Holy One of Israel, holy, glory, throne, salvation, justice, comfort, sin.

JEREMIAH
A Book of Warning

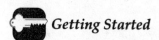 *Getting Started*

About sixty years after the death of Isaiah, God raised up another prophet for his people. A young man of twenty-one by the name of Jeremiah, from the city of Anathoth north of Jerusalem, is commissioned for what is most likely one of the hardest ministries in the Old Testament. He would have the urgent task of proclaiming God's word to Judah on the twilight of her existence as a nation. For forty years this "Weeping Prophet" preached and prophesied to a nation determined not to listen or heed his message.

When Jeremiah began his ministry, Josiah, one of the few good kings, ruled over Judah. Unfortunately, Josiah and Jeremiah were in the minority; the people were far from God and drifting further still. His ministry spanned the reign of five kings. But only Josiah feared God. "The prophets prophesy lies, the priests rule by their own authority, and my people love it this way. But what will you do in the end?" (5:31).

Jeremiah was God's mouthpiece for about fifty years in all. Most people rejected him and his message, but he remained true to his calling. His prophecies of judgment and destruction for Judah unless she repented were fulfilled. In 586 B.C. the Babylonians took the nation into captivity after levelling the city of Jerusalem and the temple. The book closes with this tragic account.

AUTHOR AND DATE

Jeremiah's name means "God sends." He was the son of the priest, Hilkiah. Jeremiah ministered between 627–575 B.C. He wrote the various parts of the book at different times during this period and from a variety of locations.

97

PURPOSE

Jeremiah's prophecy stands as a warning for all time about the divine law of reaping what you sow. Prominent in his book are the prophecies of captivity for Judah. We also get a glimpse into the heart of God himself in this book. God's heart breaks over the sin of his children; even in judgment he promises restoration.

THEME

God judges sin and rewards righteousness.

KEY VERSE

"'Return, faithless people,' declares the LORD"(3:14a).

 First Reading

Refer to the survey chart under the "Overview" section as you read the opening verse of each chapter and the segment headings printed in your Bible.

OUTLINE
A Book of Warning

    Introduction: The call of Jeremiah   1:1–19
    Sermons   2:1–20:18
        A. Public sermons   2:1–10:25
        B. Personal experience   11:1–20:18
    Later prophecies   21:1–33:26
        A. The certainty of captivity   21:1–29:32
        B. Final deliverance   30:1–33:26
    Days of fulfilment   34:1-44:30
        A. Siege and fall of Jerusalem   34:1–39:18
        B. Aftermath of the fall   40:1–44:30
    Additions   45:1–52:34
        A. God's message to Baruch   45:1–5
        B. Foreign nations   46:1–51:64
        C. Fall of Jerusalem   52:1–34

OVERVIEW

The survey chart below shows a variety of sections in the prophecy of Jeremiah. Chapters 1–44 make up the main body of the book and deal with *judgment*. A short, but bright section of *hope* appears in chapters 30–33. The book concludes with more messages of *judgment*.

CALL OF JEREMIAH	SERMONS	PROPHECIES	NARRATIVE	ADDITIONS
1	2	21	34	45 52
	Doom	Captivity and consolation	Fall of Jerusalem	
JUDGMENT				

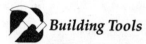 *Building Tools*

IMPORTANT SUBJECTS

The book of Jeremiah contains valuable topics for further study. Among them are:

• *The call of Jeremiah* (1:1–19). Look at the difference between God's view of the man and his perspective on himself. Also, ponder the task he was called to perform. Would you give *your* life to a ministry that bore no fruit?

• *The potter and the clay* (chapter 18). Study this chapter in regard to the sovereignty of God and also his work in your life as a Christian.

• *False shepherds* (chapter 23). Study God's stinging rebuke to those who misuse the ministry.

• *Jeremiah's rejection*. It would be difficult enough to preach without results, but God called Jeremiah to suffer rejection as well. Study the following chapters and look for evidence of rejection. Note especially *why* he was rejected: chapters 11–12,20,26,36.

KEY WORDS

unfaithful, faithless, against, turn away, return, love

LAMENTATIONS
Sad Songs About Jerusalem

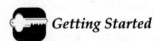 *Getting Started*

The prophet Jeremiah warned the nation of impending doom in the book that bears his name. Now, the predicted battle is history, the city vanquished and the temple toppled. The book of Jeremiah looks *ahead* to defeat, Lamentations is a *reflection* on that defeat. Lamentations is a sort of mournful "diary."

The title, Lamentations, refers to the cries and groans of the broken prophet as he looks upon the scattered bodies and shattered ruins of the smoldering city.[51]

AUTHOR AND DATE

The unnamed author was an eyewitness of the events surrounding the capture, defeat, and destruction of the city. Strong evidence points to Jeremiah. The book was obviously written soon after the destruction and siege, around 586 B.C.

PURPOSE

Jeremiah's Lamentations serves a number of obvious purposes. One purpose was to put into words for posterity the enormous sense of loss and pain the survivors felt and to admit their sin as the primary cause. Another purpose was to focus on the love and mercy of God and pray for healing and restoration in their relationship with him.

THEME

The judgment of God is swift and severe, but his mercy is available to those who repent and return to him.

---

[51] Read Jeremiah 8:19; 9:1; 14:17-22.

KEY VERSES

"Because of the LORD's great love we are not consumed, for his compassions never fail. They are new every morning; great is your faithfulness" (3:22–23).

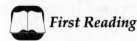 *First Reading*

Since the book of Lamentations is short, it is not difficult to scan the five chapters in one sitting. As we read, we can't help but realize its pages are filled with emotion: grief, sorrow, pain, repentance, and hope. It is the brutally honest "diary" of a broken man who identifies with the very nation he preached against.

OUTLINE

Sad Songs About Jerusalem

    A lament   1:1–4:22
        A. Jerusalem weeps   1:1–22
        B. The Lord punishes   2:1–22
        C. Hope in affliction   3:1–66
        D. Confession of sin   4:1–22
    A prayer   5:1–22
        A. "Look and see"   vv.1–10
        B. "How terrible!"   vv.11–18
        C. "Bring us back"   vv. 19–22

OVERVIEW

It is obvious that this book truly is a "lament" because the overall tone is one of grief. The writer grieves the loss of his homeland, but more so the sin of himself and his people. There is no attribution of blame on God's part, only confession of sin on the part of the writer and his people.

The survey chart below shows the five main themes addressed in the book. You will notice that there is much prayer in Lamentations. In fact, all of the last chapter is a prayer:

LAMENT				PRAYER
GRIEF 1	PUNISHMENT 2	HOPE 3	CONFESSION 4	PRAYER 5
"See how I suffer" 1:9	"He poured out his anger" 2:4	"You heard me" 3:56	"My people are cruel" 4:3	"Look and see our disgrace" 5:1

• *Grief* (1:1–22). True repentance for sin means genuine grief for sinning against God. It means admitting *personal* guilt.

• *Punishment* (2:1–22). A holy and just God *must* punish sin or compromise his righteousness.

• *Hope* (3:1–66). In the midst of punishment for sin, the hope of every true believer is the endless love and mercy of the Lord which are just as sure as his justice.

• *Confession* (4:1–22). Hope is *sure* because of the character of God, but it is *secured* through confession of sin.

• *Prayer* (5:1–22). The best fruit that can ripen in pain is sincere prayer to God. Brokenness of heart over sin is guaranteed to attract the attention and mercy of God.

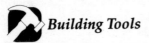 *Building Tools*

IMPORTANT PASSAGES
• *Prayers* (1:20–22; 2:20–22; 3:55–66; 5:1–22)
• *Confessions of sin* (chapters 1–2)
• *The LORD's mercies* (chapters 3–4)
• *Hope* (3:21–32; 5:9–22)

KEY WORDS
suffer(ing), comfort, cry, remember, Jerusalem

EZEKIEL
God's Message to the Captives

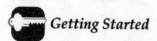 **Getting Started**

Although in fulfilment of Jeremiah's prophecy, Jerusalem was sacked in 586 B.C., the Babylonian assault on the city actually began in 605 B.C. In fact, there were *three* Babylonian invasions of Judah. Daniel was taken captive during the first invasion. Ezekiel, a twenty-six-year-old resident of Jerusalem, was taken captive during the *second* invasion[52] in 597 B.C., eleven years before the city finally fell into the hands of Nebuchadnezzar, King of Babylon, in 586 B.C.

Because of this time table, about one-half of Ezekiel's prophecy consists of the foretelling of Jerusalem's ultimate demise. The people in exile would not believe the message of doom, even as they sat captive to the very nation that Ezekiel said would conquer the city! Finally, in Nebuchadnezzar's third invasion, the city and its temple were levelled and burned.[53]

The book of Ezekiel is known for its many visions,[54] symbolic actions,[55] and picture stories.[56]

AUTHOR AND DATE

The author was Ezekiel ("God strengthens"), son of a priest, Buzi. He was called to represent God as a prophet about five years after his own capture. He wrote some time around 595–586 B.C.

PURPOSE

The primary purpose for the book of Ezekiel is to magnify God. About seventy times in the book, Ezekiel quotes the Lord,

---

[52] see 2 Kings 24:10-16
[53] see 2 Kings 25:1ff
[54] e.g. 2:9-3:3
[55] e.g. 4:1-3
[56] e.g. 15:1-8

"they will know that I am the Lord."

THEME

Restoration follows repentance in exile.

KEY VERSES

"They will know that I am the LORD, when I disperse them among the nations and scatter them through the countries" (12:15).

"You will live in the land I gave your forefathers; you will be my people, and I will be your God" (36:28).

 First Reading

This is a long book, so we should scan the forty-eight chapters first to prevent becoming lost in the details of Ezekiel's many visions. The five divisions in the book are a good starting place. Read the following five references to get a feel for the major divisions of the book: 1:1; 4:1; 25:1; 33:1; and 40:1.

OUTLINE
God's Message to the Captives

Call and commission of Ezekiel   1:1–3:27
Judgment follows sin   4:1–32:32
   A. Against Israel   4:1–24:27
   B. Against the nations   25:1–32:32
Restoration follows judgment   33:1–48:35
   A. Consolation   33:1–39:29
   B. Renewed worship   40:1–48:35

OVERVIEW

The survey chart below shows that after the opening three chapters, the book is made up of two major sections, each hinging on the theme of judgment: *Judgment follows sin* (chapters 4–32) and *Restoration follows judgment* (chapters 33–48).

CALL AND COMMISSION	JUDGMENT TO COME		RESTORATION TO COME	
	AGAINST ISRAEL	AGAINST NATIONS	CONSOLATION	RENEWED WORSHIP
1	4	25	33	40 48

• *Ezekiel's call and commission* (chapters 1–3). The book opens with God's clear call for Ezekiel to speak on his behalf to his wayward people. The "success" of his ministry is questioned from the onset.

• *Judgment follows sin* (4:1–32:32). In this section, Ezekiel documents the extent, causes and certainty of God's judgment on Judah. Ezekiel tells them it is a righteous and deserved punishment. He ends the section with a promise of global judgment some day.

• *Restoration follows judgment* (33:1–48:35). The prophet receives word in 33:21 that the city has fallen, and from that point on begins to preach a message of restoration and renewal. The book ends with the majestic affirmation, "And the name of the city from that time on will be: THE LORD IS THERE" (48:35b).

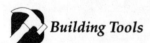 *Building Tools*

IMPORTANT PASSAGES

The book of Ezekiel contains a great deal of worthwhile themes scattered throughout its pages. The phrases in the "Key Phrases" section will also provide profitable study. Below are a few spiritual threads worth pursuing. As you read and study these passages, look for a present-day application of their truths.

- Responsibility and accountability   18:20–32
- Spiritual revival and renewal   chapter 37
- True and false prophets   chapter 13

KEY PHRASES

"Glory of the Lord," "know I am the Lord," "the word of the Lord," "vision of God," "son of man"

DANIEL
God's Man in the Government

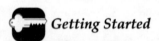 **Getting Started**

Daniel was among the first of the Jews taken into captivity by the Babylonians in 605 B.C. He lived in Babylon throughout the entire seventy-year captivity.[57] While there he was appointed as a trusted aide to King Nebuchadnezzar. God used him as his spokesman and prophet primarily to the king and the Gentile world. He was God's man in the Government. Another aspect of his ministry extended to his Jewish brethren who were with him in exile.

The book of Daniel is full of dreams and their interpretation and meaning. Very detailed descriptions of future events are depicted and cryptically explained in this book, especially the destinies of Gentile nations. Students differ over some of the *times* of fulfilment, but all agree on the prophetic events they portend. It is beyond the scope of this book to address the interpretive difficulties in the book of Daniel.

The biographical sketch in this book of Daniel himself is outstanding. He remains an example of uncompromising loyalty to God in the midst of a godless culture. The influences he faced as a young man are no less serious or damaging than those you face today. As you read and study this book, be alert for eternal principles from this man's life as well as his message.

AUTHOR AND DATE

Daniel ("God is judge") wrote this book some time after the last recorded event (10:1), around 536 B.C. He was a prophet beloved of God. Three times in the book he hears God say, "you are highly esteemed" (9:23; 10:11,19).

---

[57] compare 1:1-6 and 10:1 (which is dated 536 B.C.)

PURPOSE

The two main purposes for this book are related to global affairs and the future. Daniel writes about significant events during an era of Gentile dominance, which began when Babylon vanquished Judah and will consummate in the "last days."[58]

He also wrote to predict and briefly describe a Messianic Kingdom[59] which will follow the period of Gentile supremacy. The book of Revelation in the New Testament develops these themes in greater detail.

THEME

God controls the kingdoms of men.

KEY VERSE

"The decision is announced by messengers, the holy ones declare the verdict, so that the living may know that the Most High is sovereign over the kingdoms of men and gives them to anyone he wishes and sets over them the lowliest of men" (4:17).

 First Reading

By reading the segment headings for each of the twelve chapters of Daniel, we can get a good "feel" for the book before we read. Also, by reading its beginning and end, we can familiarize ourselves with the mood the book creates: 1:1–16 records how and why Daniel comes to be the chief character; 12:13 is the closing message he receives from God.

OUTLINE
God's Man in the Government

    The setting   1:1–21
    The destinies of nations
        A. Gentiles: Powerless to oppose God   2:1–7:28
        B. Israel: Blessed for obeying God   8:1–12:12
    Conclusion: A parting promise to Daniel   12:13

---

[58] see 2:44; 7:26; and compare with Luke 21:24b
[59] see 2:44; 7:27

OVERVIEW

The survey chart below shows the general arrangement of material for this difficult prophetic book:

		Mainly historical		Mainly prediction	
1	2		7		12
The setting		GENTILE NATIONS	8	HEBREW NATION	
		Powerless in opposing God		Blessed for obeying God	

• *The setting* (chapter 1). In this chapter we are introduced to the circumstances and people which will occupy the pages that follow.

• *Gentile nations* (chapters 2–7). This section contains stories about Daniel and the kings of Babylon, such as the story of the "Lion's Den." The outcome of Gentile history is stated: it will be destroyed.

• *The Hebrew nation* (chapters 8–12). The future events, particularly of Israel, are the subject of these chapters. Israel is portrayed as having a very bright future.

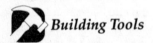

Building Tools

IMPORTANT PASSAGES

Two worthwhile themes in Daniel worth pursuing are (1) God's use of individuals, and (2) world powers and the sovereignty of God. As you carefully read through the book, be alert for insights on these two themes. Record your observations, thoughts and questions.

Another profitable study is in the familiar story of Daniel in the "Lion's Den" in chapter 6. Read the chapter slowly, even aloud. How does your life compare with his? What can you see worth emulating in Daniel?

A final study is in the account of God's servants in the fiery furnace of chapter 3. What can you learn from these young men?

KEY WORDS

Most High God, king(dom), "I saw," Nebuchadnezzar, end

HOSEA
God's Love for a Backslidden Nation

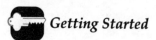 **Getting Started**

The final twelve books of our Old Testament are commonly referred to as the Minor Prophets. The "Minor" title is ascribed because of their relative brevity compared to the prophecies of Isaiah, Jeremiah, Lamentations, Ezekiel, and Daniel, the "Major Prophets." Although they are shorter, the message they carry and the importance they play are indeed "major." These twelve men all ministered to God's people during the last 350 years of Old Testament history (see chart, "Three Periods of the Prophets" on page 102). The twelve Minor Prophets can be divided into three groups based on when and to whom they spoke:

- Prophets to Israel (north): Jonah, Amos, Hosea
- Prophets to Judah (south): Obadiah, Joel, Micah, Nahum, Habakkuk, and Zephaniah
- Prophets *after* the exile: Haggai, Zechariah, and Malachi

Hosea depicts the final decay of Israel just prior to her destruction and captivity by the Assyrians in 722 B.C. (See the map on page 300 for the geography of Hosea's ministry.) His personal life is the illustration for his message; his wife becomes a harlot, just like Israel had been to God. Hosea preaches sin, judgment, and renewal like the rest of the prophets, but the momentum of iniquity is too great to be trimmed. Israel will fail to repent.

The book of Hosea is full of pathos, as we read of a faithful and godly man who must endure the pain and embarrassment of a publicly unfaithful wife, as well as the association with an ungodly and idolatrous nation.

AUTHOR AND DATE

Hosea ("salvation") was the last writing prophet to minister to the northern kingdom of Israel's ten tribes before they fell to Assyria. He was perhaps the most tender of the prophets in his contacts with Israel, being called "the prophet of the broken heart."

Hosea succeeded Amos as a prophet to Israel, so a probable date for this book is 725 B.C., shortly before the Assyrians' conquest.

PURPOSE

Hosea calls a backslidden people to return to their God to avert the impending invasion of Assyria, God's promised judgment for their infidelity.

THEME

God's love and mercy remain faithful and steadfast in the face of spiritual infidelity.

KEY VERSE

"I will heal their waywardness and love them freely, for my anger has turned away from them" (14:4).

 First Reading

First, we should scan chapters 4–14. Here we'll observe a message about Israel's adulterous relationship with the Lord. Then, scanning chapters 1–3, we will better understand God's message to the *nation* through the unusual instructions he gives to his *prophet*. We can scan by reading the first verse of each of the fourteen chapters and the section titles in our Bible.

OUTLINE
God's Love for a Backslidden Nation

The adulterous wife of a faithful husband   chapters 1–3
The adulterous nation of a faithful God   chapters 4–14
    A. The sin   chapters 4–8
    B. The judgment   chapters 9–10
    C. The restoration   chapters 11–14

OVERVIEW

The survey chart below shows the two main divisions in Hosea:

- Adulterous wife and faithful husband   chapters 1–3
- Adulterous nation and faithful God   chapters 4–14

The radical nature of Hosea's symbolic actions in the first three chapters demonstrates the corrupted nature of Hosea's marriage. Adultery and fidelity cannot coexist. In chapters 4–14 Hosea applies this principle on a deeper level to the spiritual condition of Israel in her relationship with God.[60] Hosea's message is about sin, its judgment, and God's loving work of restoration.

ADULTEROUS WIFE and FAITHFUL HUSBAND	UNFAITHFUL NATION AND FAITHFUL GOD		
1	4		
Marriage (1) Separation (2) and Reunion (3)	SIN	JUDGMENT 9	RESTORATION 11

 *Building Tools*

IMPORTANT PASSAGES

The book of Hosea contains a number of powerful themes that are sobering and comforting to us living today. Below is a list of ideas and topics to look for as you slowly and thoughtfully work your way through Hosea. Seek to better understand God's message to Israel. Then, ask God to provide you with relevant application for today:

(1) Sin—especially chapters 4–8
(2) Judgment—especially chapters 9–10
(3) Invitation to return to the Lord
(4) The promise of restoration regardless of the sin
(5) God's grace

[60] compare 3:5 with 14:8

Another fruitful study is to examine what the New Testament has to say about unfaithfulness. Following is a brief "starter" list of references: Revelation 2:4; Romans 9:22–28; 1 Peter 2:9–10; Matthew 9:13.

KEY WORDS

return, hear, heart, know(ledge), lover, love, Israel, Judah

JOEL
The Day of the Lord

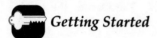 *Getting Started*

The Jews lived in an agricultural society; in fact, their lives depended upon the seasons. As a result, God frequently spoke to them in terms of nature.[61] The book of Joel opens with an account of a recent locust plague that devastated Judah. The description of the extent of damage is very graphic: grapevines stripped clean, fields levelled, and fruit trees barren. The event was fresh in the minds of all the inhabitants of the southern kingdom. Joel uses this national tragedy as a comparative basis for portraying the seriousness of the coming judgment of God. In so many words, he tells them, "If you think this locust plague was bad, you haven't seen anything yet!"

His message to them is to repent before God unleashes his judgment: an army from the north (i.e., Babylon) will descend upon Judah like the locusts if they do not turn from their wickedness.

The book follows the same format as most of the prophetical books: judgment is imminent, restoration will follow.

AUTHOR AND DATE

Joel may have lived in Jerusalem during the reign of Joash, serving as a priest when God extended his ministry to become a prophet.[62] Joel served in this capacity during the good early years of Joash's rule. If this is the time he wrote, a date of around 820 B.C. would fit. This is nearly 200 years *before* the Babylonian armies devastated Judah in 586 B.C.

---

[61] Jesus' teaching in the parables usually centred around some aspect of farming, shepherding, or vineyards.
[62] see Jeremiah 1:1

PURPOSE

Joel had both an immediate and long-term purpose. First, God wanted the Jews in Judah to know that he planned to judge their sin with great severity if they did not repent. He called them to return to him with "torn hearts" (i.e., "rend your heart and not your garments" of 2:13). A second purpose for the book of Joel was to establish a record for all nations for all time that the Day of the Lord will herald the end of human history as we know it and the events surrounding that "day." The Day of the Lord is described as the final settling of the accounts of justice.

THEME

God will some day bring human history to its just conclusion.

KEY VERSE

"And everyone who calls on the name of the LORD will be saved; for on Mount Zion and in Jerusalem there will be deliverance, as the LORD has said, among the survivors whom the LORD calls" (2:32).

 First Reading

You can read the three chapters of this short prophecy in a single sitting. As you do, watch for the "strong" language of the book as well as repeated words and phrases. You may even find it helpful to copy the basic elements of the outline below on the pages of your Bible.

OUTLINE
The Day of the Lord

    Judah   1:1–2:11
        A. Awful plague now   1:1–20
        B. The worst is yet to come!   2:1–11
    Call to repentance   2:12–27
        A. Restoration is possible   2:12–27
    Gentile nations and Israel   2:28–3:21
        A. The era of the Spirit   2:28–29
        B. The Day of the Lord   2:30–3:21
            1. Judgment on the nations   2:30–3:16a
            2. Blessings on Israel   3:16b–21

OVERVIEW

The survey chart below shows three main sections in the book of Joel: Judah; Call to Repentance; Gentile Nations and Israel (believing Jews):

JUDAH		CALL TO REPENTANCE	GENTILE NATIONS AND ISRAEL	
Awful plague now	Worse coming	Restoration possible	Spirit era	Day of the Lord
1	2:1	2:12	2:28	2:30 3:21

Descriptions and Prophecies Pointing to the Day of the Lord →

| 1:15 | 2:1 | 2:11 | | 2:31 | 3:14 |

• *Judah* (1:1–2:11). This section calls Judah to reflect on the locust plague they have just endured, and to consider that unless they repent, the judgment of God will eclipse it in devastation.

• *Call to repentance* (2:12–2:27). In this middle section, Joel announces that restoration is possible for repentant people of Judah who have strayed from God but want to return to him.

• *Gentile nations and Israel* (2:28–3:21). The last section peers into a future era of the Spirit when God will speak to Gentiles, as well as Jews. The Day of the Lord will be a time of just judgment of the nations, but believing Israel will be saved.

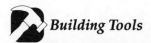 *Building Tools*

IMPORTANT PASSAGES

Three passages within Joel are especially prominent and worth extra time in studying:

• *The coming Day of Judgment* (2:1–11). Joel foresaw an invading army coming against Judah. Many years later, Jeremiah pronounced the same message, naming Babylon as Judah's enemy. What is the significance of the fact that God continued to call Judah to repent for nearly 200 years before bringing judgment?

• *The era of the Holy Spirit and the Day of the Lord* (2:28–32). Read this passage and then compare it with Peter's proclamation in Acts 2:16–21. Think of what this means for you as a Christian.

•*New life promised for Judah* (3:16–21). The predicted prospect for Judah in the end times is magnificent. As you study this passage, note especially the references to the nation, the land, and the city of Jerusalem. Think of what a message this is in an age when so many seek the destruction of Israel and its city.

KEY WORDS

locusts, Day of the Lord, cry, return, come, joy

AMOS
Prepare to Meet God

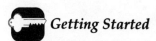 **Getting Started**

Amos spoke for God to the northern kingdom of Israel while evil Jeroboam II was king.[63] After Israel had suffered much as a nation, God provided them with a season of victory over their enemies in battle.[64] Israel was enjoying a boom. Commerce was flourishing, building was booming, and the military was enjoying the spoils of victory. Unfortunately, when the people had tasted power and wealth, they fell into sins of luxurious excess and the moral and spiritual decay that accompanies them.

To these jaded multitudes, Amos is given the assignment of preaching coming judgment for sin. Prosperity seems to dull the hearts of God's people, so Amos' task was indeed a difficult one.

AUTHOR AND DATE

The writer was Amos ("burden bearer"), a native of the city of Tekoa, just six miles south of Bethlehem in Judah. He probably penned this brief book near the end of Jeroboam's reign, around 760 B.C.

PURPOSE

Like the rest of the prophets, Amos preached to warn the northern kingdom to return to the Lord or be judged. His book presents a righteous and holy God who demands and deserves their allegiance. But also a merciful God, willing to forgive and restore them if they will only repent. This message was proclaimed with force and conviction.

---

[63] see 1:1 and 7:14–15
[64] see 2 Kings 14:25-28

THEME

Israel, prepare to meet your God!

KEY VERSE

"Therefore this is what I will do to you, Israel, and because I will do this to you, prepare to meet your God, O Israel" (4:12).

 First Reading

A quick scan of the section headings reveals clearly that the prominent theme of Amos is God's judgment. The book opens with a note of impending judgment: "He said: 'The LORD roars from Zion and thunders from Jerusalem; the pastures of the shepherds dry up, and the top of Carmel withers'" (1:2), and ends with a statement of hope: "'I will plant Israel in their own land, never again to be uprooted from the land I have given them,' says the LORD your God" (9:15). The dual message that God is holy *and* God is love abides in the pages of Amos' prophecy.

OUTLINE
Prepare to Meet God

> Judgment   1:1–9:10
>> A. Judgments against the nations   1:3–2:3
>> B. Judgments against Judah   2:4–5
>> C. Judgments against Israel   2:6–9:10
>>> 1. Sermons   2:6–6:14
>>> 2. Five visions   7:1–9:10
>
> Hope: God's patience and the promised Messiah   9:11–15

OVERVIEW

The following survey chart shows that over eight chapters of Amos' prophecy are about God's judgments for sin. The three groups that are the objects of judgment in the first section are Gentile nations, Judah, and Israel. The book concludes with a high note of *promise* for God's people.

	JUDGMENT				HOPE
Introduction	JUDGMENTS AGAINST NATIONS	JUDGMENTS AGAINST JUDAH	JUDGMENTS AGAINST ISRAEL		MESSIANIC PROMISE
	1:3	2:4	2:6	7:1	9:11 9:15
	The righteousness of God's law				The longsuffering of God's grace

• *Judgments against nations* (1:3–2:3). The Gentiles are under the judgment of God because of their sin, not because they are outside of God's "family."

• *Judgments against Judah* (2:4–5). A brief but powerful indictment against the southern kingdom. They have rejected and disobeyed the light of God's commands in favour of false gods.

• *Judgments against Israel* (2:6–9:10). This section consists of five different visions with the same theme: judgment. Mercy appears in the first two visions but is absent in the final three.

• *Long-suffering of God's grace* (9:11–15). Amos concludes with a promise to restore the kingdom of David. A near fulfilment would be Israel's return to the land from captivity; the distant fulfilment would be a kingdom without end. The eternal reign of Christ is in view.

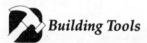 *Building Tools*

IMPORTANT PASSAGES

Examine the five visions of Amos below. What can you learn from them regarding the character of God, the nature of sin and judgment?

    (1) Locusts   7:1–3
    (2) Fire   7:4–6
    (3) Plumb line   7:7–9
    (4) Ripe fruit   8:1–14
    (5) Lord beside altar   9:1–10

KEY WORDS

sins, I will . . ., the Lord showed me, hear this word, the Lord says

OBADIAH
A Rock That Fails and a Kingdom That Endures

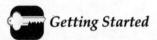 *Getting Started*

From time to time, God commissioned some of his prophets to preach to foreign nations closely involved with the history of his people. Obadiah was one such prophet. He was God's messenger to Edom, a hostile kingdom southeast of Judah, bordering on the Dead Sea (see map, "Geography of the Minor Prophets of Judah," on page 300).

The Edomites were descendants of Esau and had given Israel problems since they left Egypt under Moses' leadership.[65] They were constantly subject to their neighboring nations, so they built a fortress in the steep mountains in their area. They felt an unhealthy sense of security in their "nest" in the rocks. God tells Obadiah to predict their doom for their continual refusal to befriend Israel.

AUTHOR AND DATE

Obadiah ("servant of the Lord") was the author of this brief message of doom. He prophesied before the time of Joel, probably writing some time between 840-825 B.C.

PURPOSE

To demonstrate that those who despise Jehovah will by no means be exempt from the consequences of their unbelief. Also, this book issues a strong statement to those nations who rely on military might for security at the expense of honouring and trusting God.

---

[65] Genesis 25:19-34 gives their historical origin. Numbers 20:14-21 tells of their refusal to allow the nation of Israel to pass through their territory on the way to Canaan. Other passages that tell of Edom's involvement with Israel are 1 Samuel 14:47; 2 Samuel 8:14; and 2 Chronicles 20:1-23; 28:17.

THEME

Judgment is inevitable and ultimate, even if it is not always immediately apparent.

KEY VERSE

"The day of the LORD is near for all nations. As you have done, it will be done to you; your deeds will return upon your own head" (v. 15).

 First Reading

The book of Obadiah consists of a mere twenty-one verses— it is the shortest book in the entire Old Testament. The opening verse tells us the book's theme: the judgment of Edom. The book concludes with statements about God's people reclaiming the land taken from them and the restoration of the Lord's kingdom. We see that this is a book about vindication and justice.

OUTLINE
A Rock That Fails and a Kingdom That Endures

Title and introduction   v. 1
Edom vs. the Lord   vv. 2–14
    A. The coming destruction of Edom   vv. 1–9
    B. Edom's crimes against Judah   vv. 10–14
Day of the Lord is near   vv. 15–21
    A. Judgment of all nations   vv.15–16
    B. Restoration of Judah   vv.17–21

OVERVIEW

The survey chart shows that this book "targets" three groups: the nation of Edom, all other Gentile nations, and God's people in Judah.[66] The prophet's message to each group begins with a similar "call" to listen:

---

[66] The residents of Judah are sometimes referred to as "Israel" in Obadiah. This is because Israel is also the name given to Jacob, the father of the 12 tribes. It was not until the kingdom split in 931 B.C. that the name "Israel" was also used for the northern ten tribes and "Judah" for the 2 southern tribes.

(Edom): "This is what the Sovereign LORD says about Edom" (v. 1)

(Gentiles): "The day of the LORD is near for all nations" (v. 15)

(Judah): "Because of the violence against your brother Jacob, you will be covered with shame; you will be destroyed for ever" (v. 10).

EDOM		ALL NATIONS	GOD'S PEOPLE
1		15	17 21
Coming destruction of Edom	Cause of Edom's judgment 10	Day of the Lord near	
	Judah persecuted	Nations judged	Judah restored

• *God's message to Edom* (1–14). The destruction of Edom will be total. The cause? Her enmity and ill treatment of "your brother Jacob."

• *God's message to all nations* (15–16). Just judgment of all nations is coming.

• *God's message to Judah* (17–21). They will be restored after the captivity in Babylon, but these verses also have a much distant future glance to the end times when Mount Zion will again be a holy place and God's people will take back the cities of Judah. The last line of this prophecy resounds with a message of God's ultimate rule: ". . . And the kingdom will be the LORD's" (21b).

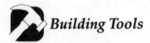 *Building Tools*

IMPORTANT PASSAGES

When Obadiah wrote this short prophecy, Edom as a nation had come to a spiritual "point of no return." That is, she was not offered any hope of salvation in this prophecy. This is not because God is unmerciful. Rather, Edom had already spurned the mercies of God. Compare Romans 1:18–32 with Edom's condition.

KEY WORDS

Edom, nations, should not . . . nor . . .

JONAH
Prophet on the Run

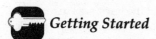 **Getting Started**

Jonah, along with Noah, is probably a "household word." His name immediately conjures up a mental image of a "large fish" and a miraculous ride! But the full story centres more around the prophet's commission from God and his responses to the Lord.

Jonah was the first of God's prophets to the northern king-dom of Israel.[67] Most of what can be known about him comes from this book that bears his name.[68] It contains his report of his mission to Nineveh, the capital city of Israel's enemy, Assyria.

The pagan Assyrians were notorious for their wickedness. Stories of their barbarous cruelty has circulated throughout the known world, and Jonah certainly knew of their atrocities. The city of Nineveh was one of the most formidable fortresses known to man. It had one hundred foot high walls with towers that reached one hundred feet higher! It has been said that the walls were so thick that three chariots could drive on top of them—side-by-side! It was surrounded by a moat that was almost 150 feet across and 60 feet deep.

It was to *this* frightening city that Jonah was called to preach judgment! It should not surprise us that instead of heading northeast to Nineveh, Jonah set a course west for Tarshish. The book of Jonah stands as one of the clearest testimonies in all of Scripture to the fact that God "so loved the world..." as we see the Lord seeking to embrace the Assyrians and spare them punish-ment. It also stands as one of the clearest witnesses in the Bible to *our* basic fear or refusal to reach out to people who we see as our "enemies."

---

[67] see 2 Kings 14:23-29
[68] Jesus refers to Jonah as a historical figure and his encounter with the "large fish" as historical as well. In fact, Jesus links his own death and burial with the historicity of Jonah's experience in Matthew 12:39-41 and Luke 11:29-30.

AUTHOR AND DATE

The traditionally accepted view is that Jonah wrote this book using the third person pronoun. Jonah ("dove") was the son of Amittai, whose family lived in the region that would one day be Jesus' home town, Nazareth. Jonah ministered some time between 785-770 B.C.

PURPOSE

This book's primary purpose, for the Jews, was to teach *their responsibility* to deliver the message of salvation to all people, Jew or Gentile, and to show them *God's willingness* to honor repentance for sin, regardless of who the sinner is.[69]

A second, less obvious, purpose for this book, was to lay down an illustration of the death, burial, and resurrection of Jesus Christ which would occur over seven centuries later.

THEME

God would rather forgive repentant sinners than punish the unrepentant.

KEY VERSE

"He prayed to the LORD, 'O LORD, is this not what I said when I was still at home? That is why I was so quick to flee to Tarshish. I knew that you are a gracious and compassionate God, slow to anger and abounding in love, a God who relents from sending calamity'" (4:2).

First Reading

This short book of four chapters can easily be read in a single sitting. Because of the familiarity of the story, we need to guard ourselves from thinking we already know all there is to know about the book of Jonah. As you read this book you will notice that it opens with Jonah's disobedience to God's call, and closes with an argument between Jonah and God. The idea of disobedience looms large in this book.

---

[69] see also Jeremiah 18:7-10; Romans 3:29 and Mark 16:15

OUTLINE
Prophet on the Run

Jonah's first commission   1:1–2:10
    A. Jonah flees   1:1–17
    B. Jonah prays   2:1–9
    C. Jonah is delivered   2:10
Jonah's second commission   3:1–4:11
    A. Jonah preaches   3:1–10
    B. Jonah complains   4:1–9
    C. God reproves   4:10–11

OVERVIEW

The survey chart clearly shows that the book falls neatly into two parts, each characterized by a "commissioning" from God. The first part ends on an encouraging note: Jonah repents, prays to God, and is delivered from the great fish. However, the second part ends on a low note in the experience of the prophet: in anger and jealousy he contends with God over his mercy toward Nineveh. This is a rare occurrence in the Bible, a book that ends with conflict and an indication of resolution.

FIRST COMMISSION		SECOND COMMISSION	
Jonah flees	Jonah prays	Jonah preaches	Jonah complains
1:1	2:1	3:1	4:1 4:11
"Get up; go to Nineveh; preach"			

• *First commission* (1:1–2:10). God's "call" is clear, unmistakable, and brief: "get up, get going, get preaching!" But Jonah refuses to preach to Gentiles and tries to run from God, but runs *into him* instead! From the belly of the "large fish" Jonah repents and is restored.

• *Second commission* (3:1–4:11). The second commission follows the same format as the first: "Get up, get going, get preaching!" Jonah obeys this time and the people of Nineveh repent and are spared. However, the story doesn't end happily, at least for

Jonah. He is angry with God's mercy to non-Jews. The book ends with God's statement that he can show mercy on whomever he will.

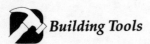 *Building Tools*

IMPORTANT PASSAGES

The book of Jonah is literally teeming with topics for study. The most obvious one is obedience. Slowly and carefully work your way through the book and pick out every instance where God commanded someone (or something, e.g., fish, worm, etc.) to *do* something. Record their responses and then compare them with Jonah, the "prophet of God."

Another study is in Jonah's prayer in chapter two. What can you learn about Jonah and God from this prayer?

Finally, examine the Gentiles' (i.e., the sailors, Ninevites, and the King) response to God compared to Jonah's (especially in the last chapter).

KEY WORDS

great city, angry, Lord

MICAH
Do What the Lord Requires of You!

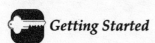 *Getting Started*

Micah was preaching to the people and leaders of Judah at the same time Isaiah and Hosea were executing their ministry to the northern kingdom of Israel. The residents of Judah were guilty of idolatry, and political, social and spiritual decay. Micah especially addressed the issue of oppression of the poor by the rich.

A portion of Micah's messages dealt with the northern kingdom. In fact, he predicted the fall of the capital city Samaria, and in 722 B.C. the Assyrian armies conquered the northern kingdom of Israel.[70] But, Micah was primarily a prophet to the southern kingdom of Judah.

AUTHOR AND DATE

Very little is known about this mighty prophet. He lived in the country town of Moresheth-gath, about twenty miles southwest of Jerusalem, and probably wrote the book around 730 B.C. It is interesting to note that Micah was a "small town boy" serving God in the south, while Isaiah was a "city boy" serving God in the north. Both of these prophets predict an essential element in the coming Messiah's life: Micah, his *birth* in 5:2, and Isaiah, his *death* in chapter 53.

PURPOSE

Micah proclaimed the "standard" prophetic message of his day: repent or judgment will come, and comfort will eventually arrive. Micah also interjects a messianic message near the end, indicating that Israel's ultimate hope lies in the distant future.

---

[70] compare Micah 1:6–7 and 2 Kings 17

THEME

Obedience is the mark of the faithful remnant of the people of God.

KEY VERSE

"He has showed you, O man, what is good. And what does the LORD require of you? To act justly and to love mercy and to walk humbly with your God" (6:8).

 First Reading

The seven chapters of Micah can be scanned in a single sitting. First, read the opening and closing paragraphs of the book. You will notice that it opens with statements about judgment, both for Israel to the north and Judah to the south. The book closes with an encouraging message about restoration. These two subjects, judgment and restoration, appear a number of times throughout the book. Then, read the section titles in your Bible to get a "feel" for the basic flow of the book.

OUTLINE
Do What the Lord Requires of You!

    God of judgment   1:1–2:13
        A. The people's corruption   1:1–2:11
        B. God's promise of deliverance   2:12–13
    God of hope   3:1–5:15
        A. The leaders condemned   3:1–12
        B. The coming kingdom   4:1–5:15
    God of pardon 6:1–7:20
        A. The Lord's complaint   6:1–7:6
        B. The Lord's forgiveness   7:7–20

OVERVIEW

The survey chart shows three primary divisions within the book, each beginning with a strong exhortation to pay attention to what is about to be said[71] but also a reoccurring couplet of *judgment* and *promise* within each of the three divisions. It will be helpful to refer to this chart as you read and study Micah.

[71]see 1:2; 3:1 and 6:1

GOD OF JUDGMENT 1:1		GOD OF HOPE 3:1		GOD OF PARDON 6:1 7:20	
Judgment	Promise 2:12	Judgment	Promise 4:1	Judgment	Promise 7:7
"Hear!"		"Listen!"		"Hear!"	

• *God of judgment* (1:1–2:12). In this opening section, Micah makes reference to three future yet certain events: the fall of Samaria to the north, the fall of Judah to the south, and the destruction of the city of Jerusalem.[72]

• *God of hope* (3:1–5:15). In this section, Micah predicts the nation's return from captivity in Babylon. But, he also speaks of the coming "king" from the city of Bethlehem, the One we now know as Jesus Christ.

• *God of pardon* (6:1–7:20). The book closes with a prayer-promise of God's total forgiveness: "You will again have compassion on us; you will tread our sins underfoot and hurl all our iniquities into the depths of the sea" (7:19).

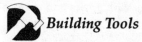 *Building Tools*

IMPORTANT PASSAGES

The couplet of *judgment* and *promise* mentioned above is a fruitful study in itself. Below are the references for each of the two themes. Read them slowly, and jot down any insights you can glean from these words of Micah:

JUDGMENT	**PROMISE**
1:2–2:11	2:12
3:1–12	4:1–5
6:1–16	7:1–20

KEY WORDS

hear, right, temple, Zion, mountain of the Lord, Jerusalem, Jacob, nations

---

[72] These events were fulfilled in 722 B.C., 702-701 B.C., and 586 B.C. respectively.

NAHUM
Woe to Nineveh!

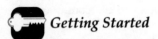 **Getting Started**

What Jonah threatened *could* happen to Nineveh if they refused to repent, Nahum promised one hundred years later *would* happen, regardless. In response to the preaching of Jonah, the Ninevites repented and were spared. But it wasn't long after, that Assyria began a downward spiral spiritually from which it would never recover.

In 722 B.C., the Assyrians invaded and destroyed the northern kingdom of Israel and in 701 B.C. they invaded Judah.[73] At this juncture in history, Assyria was drunk with power and wealth. She would not acknowledge her sin or listen to God. Her fall was the inevitable consequence of pride and destruction. God commissioned Nahum to pronounce doom on Nineveh. Not many years later, in 612 B.C., Nineveh was crushed and demolished by the Babylonians, Medes, and Scythians, never to be rebuilt again.

AUTHOR AND DATE

The prophet Nahum wrote the book that bears his name during the years 650–620 B.C.

PURPOSE

Nahum is the sequel to Jonah. It records what eventually happened to the nation God spared earlier and why. It also documents a vital principle of Scripture: Justice is sure, though not always immediate.

---

[73] read 2 Kings 17:6 and 18:13-18

THEME

God will judge the unrighteous and vindicate the righteous.

KEY VERSE

"The LORD is good, a refuge in times of trouble. He cares for those who trust in him, but with an overwhelming flood he will make an end of Nineveh; he will pursue his foes into darkness" (1:7–8).

 First Reading

This brief book can be read in a single sitting. While you read, note the repeated references to Nineveh and Assyria, Judah, and the Lord. Also, read the first couple verses of each chapter and the final two verses of the book.

OUTLINE

Woe to Nineveh!

```
The Lord's majesty    1:1–2:2
    A. Nineveh's judge    1:1–8
    B. Nineveh's fall and Judah's protection    1:9–2:2
Nineveh's destruction    2:3–3:19
    A. The fall    2:3–13
    B. The causes    3:1–19
```

OVERVIEW

The survey chart below shows the two primary divisions in the book of Nahum. The first *represents* the Lord as Judge; the second represents him *executing* his judgments.

LORD'S MAJESTY		NINEVEH'S DESTRUCTION	
1		2:3	3:19
J U S T I C E		J U D G M E N T	
Nineveh's judge	Nineveh to fall; and Judah to be protected 1:9	The Fall	The Causes 3:1

• *Nineveh's judge* (1:2–2:2). The character of Nineveh's judge is discussed, as well as the certainty of Nineveh's fall and the promise of protection to Judah.

• *Nineveh's judgments* (2:3–3:19). The last half of the book describes the destruction of Nineveh in meticulous detail:[74]

(1) They would be destroyed while they were drunk (1:10; 3:11)
(2) A flood would occur (1:8; 2:6)
(3) The city would be devastated by fire (1:10; 3:13,15)
(4) The destruction would take time (3:14)

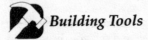 *Building Tools*

IMPORTANT PASSAGES

A number of themes in this little book are worth pursuing. One is the list of sins that Nineveh was guilty of in 3:1–19. Work your way through the list slowly, asking yourself as you go, "How are these sins evident in my culture today?" And, "What will God do about them? What should *I* do about them?"

A second theme is God's gracious statements to Judah. Look at each of the ones listed here and meditate on its message of hope: 1:12–13,15; 2:2.

---

[74] All of the above details have been supported through archaeology or ancient writing outside the Bible. When God makes a prediction about final judgment, it comes to pass!

HABAKKUK
Those Who Trust in God Will Live

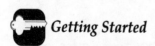 **Getting Started**

Habakkuk was the final voice of God to Judah before she was destroyed and carried off to captivity by the Babylonians. (See the chart on page 12.) He was a contemporary of Jeremiah, who lived to experience the things Habakkuk foretold.

Despite the powerful and continual ministry of the prophets, Judah had degenerated into an ungodly and idolatrous nation by the time Habakkuk addressed them.[75] His message is dripping with passion, "Why do you make me look at injustice? Why do you tolerate wrong? Destruction and violence are before me; there is strife, and conflict abounds" (1:3).

Habakkuk was frustrated with the coldheartedness of his countrymen, but he was also upset that God hadn't done anything about it yet. God responds to Habakkuk by telling him that the Babylonians are about to become his agent of justice.

AUTHOR AND DATE

What little we know about this lone prophet comes from this book. His name means "embracer" and he most likely wrote some time between 625-605 B.C., about twenty years before his prophecy was fulfilled.

PURPOSE

The book documents a number of conversations between the prophet and God. In their "talks," we are given insight about how God uses the wicked to achieve his purposes and the issue of ultimate justice.

---

[75] Second Chronicles 36:14-16 contains a good description of the spiritual condition of Judah at this time.

THEME
Any nation that trusts in itself rather than God will fall.

KEY VERSE
"See, he is puffed up; his desires are not upright—but the righteous will live by his faith" (2:4).

 First Reading

First, compare the opening and closing verses of the book, 1:2 and 3:18–19. You will immediately see a question and its conclusion. Then, scan the intervening verses. You will notice that they comprise a conversation between Habakkuk and God. Notice which parts are spoken by each.

OUTLINE
Those Who Trust in God Will Live

Habakkuk's complaints   1:2–17
     A. His first question   1:2–4
     B. God's first answer   1:5–11
     C. His second question   1:12–17
     D. God's second answer   2:1–20
Habakkuk's prayer   3:1–19

OVERVIEW
The book can be divided into three sections, as the survey chart below shows. Use the chart as you read and study:

HABAKKUK COMPLAINS 1	THE LORD ANSWERS 2	HABAKKUK PRAYS 3
Questions and answers	Decrees	Praise and testimony
"How long shall I cry out?" 1:2		"I will rejoice" 3:18

•*Habakkuk complains* (1:2–4; 12–2:1). The prophet sees evil people gaining in life while good people lose out. He contends with God that this is unfair. Habakkuk is speaking of unrighteous Jews in the first passage and unrighteous Gentiles in the second.

• *The Lord answers* (1:5–11; 2:2–20). God's response is that justice will be served. He tells the prophet that any nation that is evil and self-serving will fail.

•*Habakkuk prays* (3:1–19). The prophet's personal dilemma is resolved. He opened the book with an accusing question, but he closes this book with a ringing affirmation of trust and praise.

 *Building Tools*

IMPORTANT PASSAGES

Without doubt, the prayer of Habakkuk in chapter 3 is worth further study. Read it carefully, taking note of his description of God's character and the results in his own life of contemplating it. His closing prayer is one of the most moving in all of the Bible. Try to compose one like it yourself and then pray it back to God.

Another short study is to follow Habakkuk's statement in 2:4 into the New Testament where it is quoted three times: Galatians 3:11; Romans 1:17 and Hebrews 10:38. Study the New Testament usage of Habakkuk's words to give you a fuller understanding of what they meant to the Jew of his day.

KEY WORDS

Lord, how long? why?

ZEPHANIAH
Desolation and Deliverance

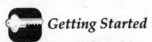 **Getting Started**

By now, it is obvious that the recurring characters in the Minor Prophets are: the Lord, his people (Judah and Israel), and the Gentile nations. The recurring themes are: judgment, repentance, and restoration. Zephaniah accomplishes all of the above in fifty-three short verses, and does so in a stinging fashion nearly unequalled in the entire Old Testament!

Zephaniah was a prophet to Judah during the reign of Josiah, last of the kingdom's righteous rulers. At age twenty, Josiah began a six-year programme of national reform.[76] The sins which Zephaniah condemns in this book were the very sins over which the nation's righteous king lamented.

Zephaniah prophesied judgments for Jerusalem that began to fall within a half a century. The same prophecies refer to judgment of end times, followed by restoration of the Jews who repented of their rejection of the Messiah. Zephaniah writes of a great "Day of the Lord," which will come with fury and force, and the aftermath of that "day."

AUTHOR AND DATE

Zephaniah ("protected by the Lord") wrote this book during the term of his public ministry as a prophet of God, around 635–625 B.C. He may have been a descendant of the good king, Hezekiah.

PURPOSE

The book of Zephaniah speaks of the "Day of the Lord," a time of grief and pain for those who have rejected God, but a time of blessing and praise for those who love him.

---

[76] Read 2 Chronicles 34 and 35.

THEME

Judgment will come. Where will you stand?

KEY VERSE

"The great day of the LORD is near—near and coming quickly. Listen! The cry on the day of the LORD will be bitter, the shouting of the warrior there. That day will be a day of wrath, a day of distress and anguish, a day of trouble and ruin, a day of darkness and gloom, a day of clouds and blackness" (1:14–15).

 First Reading

Read the book through in a single sitting. How does it compare with the other Minor Prophets you have read? Read the opening and closing paragraphs. What can you glean about God's character from them?

OUTLINE
Desolation and Deliverance

> Judgment   1:1–2:3
>> A. For everyone   1:1–3
>> B. For Judah   1:4–13
>> C. For the whole world   1:14–18
>> D. Repent!   2:1–3
> Punishment and destruction   2:4–3:8
>> A. For the nations   2:4–15
>> B. For Jerusalem   3:1–8
> Believers' salvation   3:9–20

OVERVIEW

The survey chart shows that Zephaniah has three major subject divisions: Judgment, Punishment, and Salvation. Use the chart below as you read and study:

JUDGMENT				PUNISHMENT		SALVATION	
All	Judah	Whole world	CALL TO REPENTANCE	For nations	For Jerusalem	New day for God's people	
1:1	1:4	1:14	2:1	2:4	3:1	3:9	3:20

• *Judgment* (1:1–2:3). This section predicts fierce judgment for the world and everything in it, and the inhabitants of Jerusalem. It concludes with a call to repent.

• *Punishment* (2:4–3:8). Again, the whole world and Jerusalem are in view. The punishment spoken of here is complete and thorough, not a mere chastening.

• *Salvation* (3:9–20). At the end of time, Jerusalem will be the centre of God's kingdom on earth. All of its inhabitants will be believers. The statements here parallel those of the apostle John nearly seven hundred years later (Revelation 20:4–6).

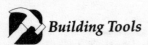 *Building Tools*

IMPORTANT PASSAGES

Two passages within Zephaniah are excellent for study. One is the description of the "Day of the Lord" in 1:14–2:3. Read it carefully and keep telling yourself that this is actually going to happen . . . possibly in *your* lifetime! The second passage is Zephaniah's vision of the final Jerusalem in chapter 3. Study this carefully as well, realizing that you will spend eternity there. What thoughts have come to you as you've examined these two passages? Perhaps it would be good to spend some time with God right now in worship and adoration.

Finally, look at 2 Peter 3:10–14. What additional thoughts does Peter add to your study about the end times, especially as it relates to your own life and conduct right now?

KEY WORDS

"declares the Lord," ". . . day . . .," "I will . . .," destroy, rejoice

HAGGAI
The Temple Is Rebuilt

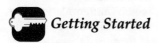 *Getting Started*

It is difficult for us to imagine the sight that greeted those returning from captivity in Babylon. When they had been deported, their city was under siege. When they returned, it was under ruins. The walls were broken down, the city demolished and ashen, but most tragically, their temple was in ruins. The confrontation with the consequences of their persistent disobedience was probably more than many could bear.

Haggai was among the first group of Jews that returned to Jerusalem from Babylon in 536 B.C.[77] The people started the enormous task of rebuilding the temple, but soon opposition from outsiders discouraged them to the point of quitting altogether.[78] Fourteen years later, around 520 B.C., when Haggai wrote his book, the temple project was still stymied.

The people, once discouraged, had since become self-satisfied, neglecting the things of God in favour of personal pursuits. They were building nice homes for themselves, and few grieved that the God of Israel didn't having a dwelling place. So, God raised up Haggai and Zechariah to stir them up, urging them to resume the rebuilding of God's temple.

The people responded, and in 516 B.C. they completed the task. We know from the book of Ezra that the Temple's completion was a direct result of the ministry of Haggai and Zechariah, "So the elders of the Jews continued to build and prosper under the preaching of Haggai the prophet and Zechariah, a descendant of Iddo" (Ezra 6:14a).

---

[77] see Ezra 1:5-2:70 and Nehemiah 12
[78] see Ezra 4:1-5,24

AUTHOR AND DATE

The author Haggai ("festival of God") was probably a Babylonian-born Jew. He and Zechariah were companions in the prophetic ministry.[79] This book was written around 520 B.C., sixteen years after the first pilgrimage from Babylon to Jerusalem.

PURPOSE

Haggai reminds the Jews (and us!) that God is a person and, as such, demands a "place" in our lives. The temple was the visible "place" of God's personal contact with his people. The Jews needed this central spiritual edifice to remind them of God's presence.

THEME

The things of God must have priority over the things of self.

KEY VERSE

"'Go up into the mountains and bring down timber and build the house, so that I may take pleasure in it and be honoured,' says the LORD" (1:8).

 First Reading

This is a short book of only two chapters. Read it through twice in a single sitting if possible. Look for repeated words and phrases.

OUTLINE
The Temple Is Rebuilt

The charge to resume building   1:1–11
The work is begun   1:12–15
Encouragement to finish the work   2:1–23
    A. Encouragement   2:1–9
    B. Blessing   2:10–19
    C. Zerubbabel honoured   2:20-23

---

[79] see Ezra 5:1 and 6:14

OVERVIEW

Once again the book falls neatly into three divisions: Charge to begin building, building, and encouragement to finish building.

Use the chart below to assist you as you read and study Haggai. As you do, be attentive to every reference to the Lord. How does he show the people the priority of building the temple over their *own* building projects?

CHARGE TO RESUME BUILDING 1:1	WORK BEGUN 1:12	ENCOURAGEMENT TO FINISH 2:1 2:23
"My house is still in ruins!"	"People were excited"	"I will bless"

• *Charge to resume building* (1:1–11). The people try to convince themselves that now is not the "right time" to resume building. God rebukes this idea swiftly through Haggai.

• *Building* (1:12–15). It is interesting to notice the positive effect the excitement of the *leaders* had on the followers! The people actually become anxious to finish the temple.

• *Encouragement to finish building* (2:1–23). In a variety of ways God provides the necessary encouragement for his people not to give up but to finish the task. One of them is to help them reflect on its former beauty and God's presence there.

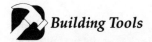 *Building Tools*

IMPORTANT PASSAGES

The first chapter of Haggai contains many valuable principles about proper priorities for God's people. Read the chapter slowly and carefully. Record all that you can about proper priorities.

Another fruitful study is God's encouragement to his people in chapter two. Do a similar study on encouragement from these verses. How does God encourage us? What can we learn from these verses about encouraging others?

KEY WORDS

temple, glory, word of the Lord, Lord Almighty, spirit

ZECHARIAH
King Over the Whole World

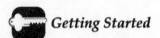 **Getting Started**

Zechariah is the longest of the Minor Prophets. He preached a message of encouragement to the temple rebuilders who had returned with him under the leadership of Zerubbabel in 536 B.C. At the time God began to reveal to Haggai the message he was to proclaim, Zechariah was serving the Lord as a priest. But soon, the Lord called him to the ministry of prophet as well. While Haggai had both feet firmly planted in the *present*, Zechariah and his message gaze toward the *future*. Haggai prods the people to use their *hands*; Zechariah encourages them to open their *hearts*. Haggai is concerned about the *physical* dwelling place of God— the temple in Jerusalem; Zechariah's passion is for God's *spiritual* abode—the hearts of his people.

Zechariah was often quoted by the New Testament writers, undoubtedly because of the strong Messianic theme in this book.

AUTHOR AND DATE

Zechariah ("the Lord remembers"), the grandson of Iddo, wrote this book sometime around 520 B.C. after the first return to Jerusalem.

PURPOSE

The immediate goal of Zechariah's prophecy is to bring about spiritual revival and to motivate and encourage the people to complete the temple. But a second reason God gave us the book of Zechariah was to officially "register" some unmistakable prophecies about the coming Messiah. Here are some examples:

PROPHECY ABOUT THE MESSIAH	FULFILMENT IN JESUS CHRIST
He would be a king-priest 6:13	Hebrews 6:20–7:1
He would be a lowly king 9:9–10	Matthew 21:4–5; John 12:13–16
He would be betrayed 11:12–13	Matthew 27:9
His hands would be pierced 12:10	John 19:37
He would come a second time and be crowned king 14:5,9	Revelation 11:15; 21:27

THEME

For the present there is pain for God's people, but a day will come when they will worship their Lord in his city, Jerusalem, for ever.

KEY VERSES

"This is what the LORD says: 'I will return to Zion and dwell in Jerusalem. Then Jerusalem will be called the City of Truth, and the mountain of the LORD Almighty will be called the Holy Mountain' . . . The LORD will be king over the whole earth. On that day there will be one LORD, and his name the only name" (8:3 and 14:9).

 First Reading

Before we seek to scan this rather long book, it will help us to study the survey chart in the "Overview" section opposite. The book can be divided into five sections. The opening verses of each section are an excellent place to begin our scan: 1:1; 1:7; 6:9; 7:1; 9:1. Then, read the section titles for the book in your Bible.

OUTLINE
King Over the Whole World

The way of salvation 1:1–6
Eight visions: Israel in history 1:7–6:8
The Bringer of salvation: "The Branch" 6:9–15
Four messages: A testimony to the world 7:1–8:23
The city of salvation: Jerusalem 9:1–14:21

OVERVIEW

The survey chart below shows two sections of the Lord speaking to Zechariah: eight visions and four messages. These two sections are surrounded by the subject of salvation: The way of salvation, the Bringer of salvation, and the city of salvation. The two comings of the Messiah and the nation of Israel also appear throughout the book.

WAY OF SALVATION 1:1	EIGHT VISIONS 1:7	BRINGER OF SALVATION 6:9	FOUR MESSAGES 7:1	CITY OF SALVATION 9:1 14:21
"Return unto me."	Israel in history	"Branch"	Testimony to the world	"Jerusalem"
	"My Temple will be rebuilt."		"We have heard that God is with you."	

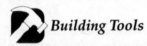

Building Tools

IMPORTANT PASSAGES

Below are four subjects in the book of Zechariah for further study. Most of it focuses on Israel and the end times:

(1) The eight visions of Israel in prophecy (1:7–6:8). This is an extended discussion of what the future holds for national Israel.
(2) Fasting (7:1–8:23)
(3) Israel's history in the end times (9:1–11:17)
(4) The King over all (12:1–14:21). When the Jews repent of their sins, God will bring them into the kingdom of his Son.

KEY WORDS

shepherd, king, Branch, Jerusalem, Israel, there before me, Lord Almighty

MALACHI
Will a Man Rob God?

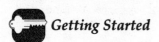 **Getting Started**

One can't help but wonder how Israel would have reacted had they known that the book of Malachi was going to be the last word from God for four hundred years! Because it was. From the time this book was written until the coming of John the Baptist would be about four hundred "silent" years.

When Malachi penned this book, the Jews as a nation had been back in Canaan for nearly one hundred years. The promised blessings of Haggai and Zechariah had not yet arrived. The Jews were discouraged and disappointed. The promises their grandparents had told them about seemed to be nothing more than old legends. Their faith and worship were slowly eroding and it was beginning to surface in their day-to-day relationships as well. God is willing to talk with his people, but tragically, their hearts are hardened by sin and they respond in like fashion.

AUTHOR AND DATE

Malachi ("my messenger") was a contemporary of the leader Nehemiah and shared his burden over the backslidden condition of the nation. He probably wrote this book around 433 B.C., the time of Nehemiah's visit to Babylon recorded in Nehemiah 13:6.

PURPOSE

Malachi wrote in an attempt to confront the people with their sin and call them back to God. He sought to balance their accountability to the Law of Moses with the unchanging love of God.

THEME

The Lord does not change. That means both his mercy *and* his holiness are operative.

145

KEY VERSES

"Surely the day is coming; it will burn like a furnace. All the arrogant and every evildoer will be stubble, and that day that is coming will set them on fire," says the LORD Almighty. "Not a root or a branch will be left to them" (4:1).

"They will be mine," says the LORD Almighty, "in the day when I make up my treasured possession. I will spare them, just as in compassion a man spares his son who serves him" (3:17).

 First Reading

First, read the opening and closing verses of the book: 1:1–2a and 4:4–6. Then, scan the four chapters for first impressions. The most obvious thing we notice as we scan is that the book consists of a conversation between the Lord and the Israelites (even though God speaks both parts).

OUTLINE
Will a Man Rob God?

    Sin   1:1–3:15
        A. God's love rejected   1:1–5
        B. The sins of the priest   1:6–2:9
        C. The sins of the people   2:10–3:15
    Blessing or punishment   3:16–4:3
    Invitation and warning   4:4–6

OVERVIEW

The Lord's messages to Israel via Malachi were *charges* for their sins, *replies* to their defences, *warnings* of judgement for sinners and *promises* of hope for those who repent.

The bulk of this prophecy is "forthtelling" (speaking on behalf of God) rather than foretelling (predicting the future). The chart below shows the dominance of the forthtelling:

S I N	PUNISHMENT OR BLESSING	INVITATION AND WARNING
1:1	3:16	4:4 4:6
Love spurned		Grace still offered

• *Sin* (1:1–3:15). In this section, God accuses the Jews of spurning his love and singles out the priests who were not honouring him as they should. He also indicts them on the charge of trying to "rob" God by withholding their tithes. This section contains a classic passage on the "forerunner" to the Messiah's first coming, which we now know to be John the Baptist.

• *Punishment or blessing* (3:16–4:3). In powerful and penetrating language, the Lord spells out the destiny of those who honour him and those who don't.

• *Invitation and warning* (4:4–6). The book ends with mention of a "curse." Perhaps a fitting way to conclude the Old Testament—a reminder of man's need to be brought out from under the curse of sin!

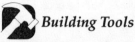 *Building Tools*

IMPORTANT PASSAGES

God accuses the nation of Israel seven times in this short book. Look up the references below and write out what the charge is and the people's response to God:

• *God's accusations*: 1:2; 1:6; 1:7; 2:17; 3:7; 3:8; 3:13.

Another good study is to examine the specific sins God charges the priests with in chapter two. List as many as you can, and jot down why you think God was so incensed over them. Also, a number of "social" sins of the people are mentioned in this same chapter. Do a similar study of them.

KEY WORDS

messenger, Lord Almighty, day, you ask...

The Old Testament: Concluding Remarks

You have completed God's Old Testament book about himself, his created universe, and his method of saving sinful mankind. Over and over again you witnessed the fact that nations and individuals were saved and delivered from judgment by faith in God as Lord and Deliverer. You also learned from books like Isaiah that this salvation is possible through the work of his servant, the Messiah, who would some day come into human history. He would die as a substitutionary sacrifice for sinners, to pay the penalty for their sins. Then he would live again and finally one day rule over his people for ever. That is the story of the Old Testament.

For four hundred years after Malachi wrote his moving book, God did not inspire the writing of any other scriptures. The thirty-nine books of the old Testament that you have read and studied were God's total written revelation during that time. God was preparing his world for the coming of his Son, the Messiah, the central promise of the Old Testament.

Then it happened, Jesus actually came, to live and die for the sins of the world. After that, God inspired new writers to complete the Bible by telling the New Testament story of Jesus and what his coming means for us. As you continue on in your reading and studying of the New Testament, be sure to keep the truths you have gleaned from the Old Testament close at hand for they are the foundation upon which the pages you are about to read are built.

The New Testament

The New Testament continues and fulfils God's message in the Old Testament. Christianity didn't just "happen." God had been working among the people of the world, especially Israel, for many centuries before Christ. Then, "when the time had fully come, God sent his Son" (Galatians 4:4). The rest of the story of God's plan for humanity is the message of the New Testament. The Old Testament is the promise; the New Testament the fulfilment.

KEY TRUTHS OF THE NEW TESTAMENT

There are key truths underlying all the details of the New Testament text. We find these truths constantly reappearing as we study the New Testament books:

1. Sin is man's basic, desperate problem.
2. Christ's payment for sin is the heart of the gospel.
3. The human race has no hope outside of God's grace.
4. The gospel is God's message to the whole world.
5. The *work* of Christ depends upon the *person* of Christ.
6. The main reason for miracles is to show Christ, the Miracle Worker.
7. The Holy Spirit is actively working in this age.
8. All world history moves toward the last days.
9. The final event of history will be when God places Jesus Christ on the throne as ruler over all (Philippians 2:9–11).
10. The New Testament gives God's full directions for living a life that is pleasing to him.

MATTHEW
Jesus the King

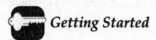 *Getting Started*

When we read or study the books of the New Testament, it helps to picture ourselves living back in the first century, when the books were actually written. Matthew is an excellent place to begin reading or studying the New Testament, not only because it is the first of the New Testament books, but also because it ties together the Old and New Testaments.

Many religious Jews of the first century wanted to know who this "Jesus" was—was he truly the Messiah, the Anointed One, the Christ foretold in *their* scriptures, our Old Testament? They had faithfully studied their Hebrew Scriptures which predicted a new kingdom to come, and now they had the opportunity to read what one of their own, a man named Matthew, had to say. He often quoted their Scriptures in his Gospel. We can only imagine their joy and excitement to read in Matthew over and over again that the things *they* saw and heard were "just as the prophets wrote"!

AUTHOR AND DATE

The author of this Gospel is Matthew, a Jewish tax collector who became a disciple of Jesus.[80] Tax collectors were despised by the Jews because they helped to perpetrate the cruel oppression of Israel through the enforcement of unjust and often illegal taxation. Most Jews would have considered Matthew a "traitor." This makes Jesus' selection of him as a disciple all the more significant.

Matthew's Gospel was probably composed in the late fifties or sixties A.D. We can surmise this because the Jewish temple

---

[80] Matthew 10:3

was destroyed by the Roman commander Titus in A.D. 70 and Matthew certainly would have mentioned it in his Gospel if it had recently occurred.

FIRST READERS

Matthew especially had the Jews in mind when he wrote his account of Jesus, but he also wrote for non-Jews as well. The world in which Matthew lived was very metropolitan and he knew that many would find themselves searching the content of his account.

PURPOSE

Matthew's primary purpose, which gave his Gospel its distinctive quality, was to show his Jewish first readers that Jesus is the king of God's promised kingdom foretold in the Hebrew Scriptures, the Old Testament.

THEME

Jesus is the promised king of the kingdom of God.

KEY VERSE

"Where is the one who has been born king of the Jews? We saw his star in the east and have come to worship him" (Matthew 2:2).

 First Reading

The opening and closing of Matthew's Gospel help reveal something about its purpose. In the opening verse we see three names: Jesus Christ, David and Abraham. These are important names in Jewish history. In the closing verses (28:19–20), notice the words "all nations" and "world." This is vital too because Matthew has been writing mainly to Jewish first readers about the Jews' Messiah. But now, we discover that Jesus had instructed *them* to share this Messiah with the whole world.

OUTLINE
Jesus the King

Jesus and His Promised Kingdom
    A. Birth and preparation of the King   1:1–4:11
    B. Message and ministry of the King   4:12–16:20
    C. Death and resurrection of the King   16:21–28:20

OVERVIEW

The book of Matthew "breaks" conveniently into three parts:

1:1 PRESENTATION	4:12 PROCLAMATION	16:21 PASSION 28:20

• *Presentation* (1:1–4:11). These chapters show how Jesus makes his "entrance" into the world of men.

• *Proclamation* (4:12–16:20). We see the opening of Jesus' public ministry in verse 4:12. We learn of Jesus' main activity during this period in 4:17, "From that time on Jesus began to preach." That is why the middle section of this overview is called "proclamation." Three of Jesus' five teaching sessions are reported in this section. Among them are Jesus' stories called parables, his favourite way of teaching.[81] As we read these chapters we can learn a great deal about who Jesus is and what he considers important for us.

• *Passion (sufferings)* (16:21–28:20). The opening verse tells us that a new section is coming up: "From that time on Jesus began to explain to his disciples that he must go to Jerusalem."[82] In the last part of that verse Jesus tells what will happen to him in Jerusalem. He will suffer, be killed, and be raised from death on the third day. The three parts of this section are Jesus' final ministries (chapters 19–23); his teachings about the end of the world (chapters 24–25) and his death and resurrection (chapters 26–28).

A quick "scan" of the life of Jesus can be done by reading the italicized headings over the sections in your Bible that contain the Gospel of Matthew (if your version of the Bible has them).

---

[81] Matthew 13
[82] Matthew 16:21

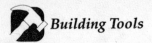 *Building Tools*

IMPORTANT PASSAGES

Most of the text of Matthew is a story line, or narrative, followed by larger sections of Jesus' teachings. This arrangement appears five times in Matthew's Gospel. Each teaching section closes with the same statement, "When Jesus had finished saying these things," or a similar statement.

Below is a list of the five teaching sections. For further study, read them slowly, taking notes as you do. Some things to look for in your study of these teaching sections are:

- Jesus' style—Does he vary it according to his audience?
- People's response—Does it vary? Why? How would you have responded?
- Jesus' message—What does it mean for us today?

THE FIVE TEACHING SECTIONS OF MATTHEW

Sermon on the Mount	chapters 5–7
Teaching the twelve apostles	chapter 10
Stories about the kingdom	chapter 13
Life in God's kingdom	chapter 18
The end of the world	chapters 24–25

KEY WORDS

kingdom, fulfilled, righteous, worship, Father

MARK
Jesus the Servant

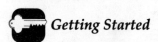 **Getting Started**

Jesus' ministry involved travelling from place to place, so he was grateful for the kindness of friends for meals and a place to sleep. While in Jerusalem he may have stayed in the house of a lady named Mary, who opened her home to believers.[83] Jerusalem was a city that throbbed and pulsed with activity and people. It was a place where peoples' needs always outweighed the assets to meet them. Young John Mark, normally known as Mark, could have been the son of this gracious woman. If so, as a teenager, he surely must have been attracted to this special guest, a man of active service to the people around him.

AUTHOR AND DATE

The writer of this second Gospel was John Mark, son of Mary and cousin of Barnabas, who was a leader in the early church.[84] Mark also travelled with the apostle Paul and was one of the last to see him alive.[85] Mark wasn't called to be one of the original twelve apostles, but he became a very close friend of the apostle Peter.[86] It was undoubtedly from Peter's first-hand reports of Jesus' life and ministry that Mark wrote his Gospel.

The actual date of composition of Mark's Gospel isn't known. Scholars vary as to date, from early (A.D. 50–64) to late (A.D. 65–70), although many believe it was the *first* of the four Gospels to be written. Portions of Mark's Gospel can be found in Matthew and Luke, possibly indicating that they used him as one of their sources.

---

[83] Acts 12:12-17
[84] Acts 12:12; Colossians 4:10
[85] 2 Timothy 4:11
[86] 1 Peter 5:13

157

FIRST READERS

Mark originally wrote his Gospel for Gentile (non-Jewish) readers in general, and the Romans in particular. The Roman mind was impressed more by action and power than by preaching and talk. The fact that Mark grew up in Jerusalem, a Roman-occupied city, made him well-suited for the special "twist" that God wanted on this particular Gospel. His natural style was to write a Gospel that was active and fast-paced, which is one of the distinctive characteristics of the Gospel of Mark.

PURPOSE

Mark wrote to portray Jesus as a man of action and power to a people who respected those traits.

THEME

Jesus Christ came into the world to offer his life as a sacrifice to save mankind.

KEY VERSE

"For even the Son of Man did not come to be served, but to serve, and to give his life as a ransom for many" (10:45).

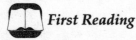 *First Reading*

In comparing the opening and closing verses of this Gospel, we discover something significant. Why does Mark open with words, "This is the beginning of the gospel"(1:1)? What is happening to the gospel in the last two verses of the book?

OUTLINE
Jesus: The Servant

Jesus: The Servant of God
    A. Jesus shows who he is through serving   1:1–8:26
    B. Jesus asks others who he is   8:27–30
    C. Jesus proves who he is through sacrifice
        8:31–16:20

OVERVIEW

The book of Mark, like the other three Gospels, is the story of selected parts of Jesus' life. Mark's account emphasizes a key turning point in Jesus' life. Read Mark 8:27–30 now and look for key words and phrases.

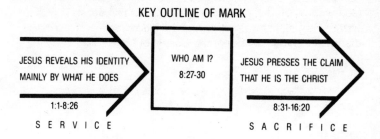

KEY OUTLINE OF MARK

JESUS REVEALS HIS IDENTITY MAINLY BY WHAT HE DOES

1:1-8:26

S E R V I C E

WHO AM I?
8:27-30

JESUS PRESSES THE CLAIM THAT HE IS THE CHRIST

8:31-16:20

S A C R I F I C E

• *Jesus acts* (1:1–8:26). This section is full of the activities of Jesus in which he demonstrates who he is by his miracles. He does not, however, plainly tell the people or his disciples that he is the Messiah, nor does he tell them what awaits him in Jerusalem.

• *Jesus asks* (8:27–30). This passage is the "hinge" of the book. Here Jesus asks his disciples some penetrating questions about himself, most notably, "Who do people say I am?" and "Who do *you* say I am?" It is here that Peter makes the reply that echoes throughout history, "You are the Christ."

• *Jesus authenticates* (8:31–16:20). In this final section, Jesus begins to unravel in word and deed, what it *means* that he is "the Christ." He first tells them plainly what lies ahead for him (8:32) and then begins his final journey to Jerusalem, stating again and again that indeed he *is* the Christ. This section is a story of sacrifice.

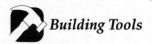

Building Tools

IMPORTANT PASSAGES

Read over the following portions of the final section of Mark's Gospel, paying special attention to the four portraits of Jesus the Servant that they contain. Jot down all the observations you make for each portion:

- Jesus as Redeemer (to buy back)   8:31–10:52
- Jesus as Lord (the Ruler over all)   11:1–13:37
- Jesus as Sacrifice (to give up his life)   14:1–15:47
- Jesus as Victor (to win over death, sin, and the devil) 16:1–20

KEY WORDS

serve [87] save, then [88]

---

[87] The word is translated "minister" in the King James Version.
[88] The word translated "then" in the NIV has the meaning of "immediately." This illustrates the theme of activity which permeates Mark's account.

LUKE
Jesus the Son of Man

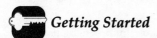 **Getting Started**

For many years after Jesus' ascension into heaven, his followers did not have any complete, God-inspired written account of his life, message and ministry. Then, in God's timing, men moved by the Holy Spirit wrote what were to become the very Gospels we have today. Although there were already a number of written accounts in existence (Mark's was one of them!), God apparently wanted us to have a Gospel that was more thorough than the others, contained more information,[89] and was characterized by meticulous detail. The man we know simply as "Luke" was God's choice for the job. You will notice in scanning Luke's Gospel that it is longer than the other three (Matthew's Gospel contains more chapters, but less actual text). In fact, the Gospel of Luke is the longest book in the entire New Testament.

AUTHOR AND DATE

This third Gospel was written by a Greek Christian named Luke. Like Mark, he was not a personal disciple of Jesus during his earthly ministry. But also like Mark, he was an intimate acquaintance with one who was an apostle. We know from other Scriptures that he was the personal physician, faithful friend, and travelling companion of the apostle Paul.[90] It is possible that Luke actually was converted under Paul's ministry while living in Antioch.[91]

---

[89] About one-half of the information found in Luke is not found in the other three Gospels.
[90] Colossians 4:14 indicates he was a doctor. Acts 16:10; 20:6; 27:1 and 28:16 indicate that Luke was a travelling companion with Paul (e.g. "us"). Second Timothy 4:11 demonstrates his intense loyalty to Paul.
[91] Acts 11:25–26

Because of Luke's unusually sensitive treatment of women and his extensive references to prayer in his Gospel, we may conclude that he too, like his Lord, was a kind and humble man of prayer with a sympathetic heart for all people in need.

Luke also wrote the book of Acts. In fact, Luke and Acts are usually viewed as volumes I and II of the same story.

It is generally accepted that Luke wrote his Gospel around A.D. 60, near the end of Paul's missionary journeys.

FIRST READERS

Luke's Gospel is addressed to an unknown man named Theophilus, whose name means "friend of God." Yet, we can also surmise that Luke wrote with his fellow Greeks (i.e., non-Jews) in mind. This is evidenced by the fact that he makes a great effort to provide explanations for various Jewish customs and feasts in his Gospel, and also periodically substitutes Greek equivalents for Hebrew names.

It could safely be said that Matthew wrote primarily for the Jews, Mark for the Romans, and Luke for the Greeks.

PURPOSE

Luke expressly states his purpose in writing, namely to provide a thorough and orderly account of the life and ministry of Jesus Christ using eyewitnesses as his primary sources.[92]

THEME

Jesus, the Son of Man among men, loves mankind and offers God's salvation from their sin.

KEY VERSE

"For the Son of Man came to seek and to save what was lost" (Luke 19:10).

 First Reading

Chapter 1 praises God joyfully in the songs of Mary (1:45–55) and Zechariah (1:67–79) in anticipation of the birth of Jesus and his forerunner, John the Baptist. In the closing verses of Luke, we

---

[92] Luke 1:1-4

again find joy and happiness with the jubilant followers of Jesus praising God in the temple all the time (24:50–53). This atmosphere of joy and praise will appear time and again as you read and study Luke's Gospel.

OUTLINE
Jesus the Son of Man

The Son of Man Among Men
A. Preparation   1:1–4:13
B. Signs   4:14–9:50
C. Teaching   9:51–19:27
D. Sacrifice   19:28–24:53

OVERVIEW

The *words* and *deeds* of Jesus are the two subjects Luke writes most about. This is captured for us at the end of his Gospel account in the words of the two men walking to Emmaus, "He was a prophet, powerful in word and deed before God and all the people" (24:19).

Below are the four main sections in the Gospel of Luke:

LUKE: SON OF MAN AMONG MEN

1:1 PREPARATION	4:14 IDENTIFICATION	9:51 INSTRUCTION	19:28 SACRIFICE 24:53
	miracles abound here—what Jesus DID	stories abound here—what Jesus SAID	

• *Preparation* (1:1–4:13). This is about getting the people ready for Jesus' coming, through John's ministry, and Jesus' preparation for his own public ministry.

• *Signs* (4:14–9:50). Jesus wanted to convince the people that he was the Messiah—the *Son of God* coming with great power and the *Son of Man* coming with concern for lost sinners. Look for signs of power and love in this section.

• *Teaching* (9:51–19:27). This section is filled with the stories (parables) of Jesus. He wanted the people to see that the Son of Man came to find lost people and save them (19:10). It hurts us to see love rejected. "All the people saw this and began to mutter, 'He has gone to be the guest of a sinner'"(19:7).

• *Sacrifice* (19:28–24:53). All the Gospels close on the moving themes of Jesus' death, resurrection and last words. Read this section slowly, thinking carefully about the *cost* to the Son of Man for their salvation and yours.

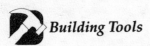 *Building Tools*

IMPORTANT PASSAGES

There are a variety of thoroughly exciting themes to study in the Gospel of Luke. Below are a few suggestions. As you approach them, be especially on the lookout for:

- Jesus' treatment of *people*, particularly the lowly
- Jesus' relationship with the Father, especially as it relates to prayer

THE SON OF MAN AMONG MEN

The disciples	6:20–23
A sinful woman	7:36–50
Mary Magdalene	8:2
The Samaritans	10:25–37
Tax collectors and "sinners"	15:1–7
Lepers	17:11–19
A thief on the cross	23:39–43

THE SON OF MAN AND PRAYER

Parables about prayer	11:5–8
	18:1–8
	18:9–14
Examples of prayer	9:28–29
	11:1–4
	22:31–32
	22:39–46

KEY WORDS

Son of Man, love, sinners, praise

JOHN
Jesus the Son of God

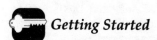 **Getting Started**

When the apostle John wrote his Gospel, many years had passed since the other three accounts had been penned. Matthew had written to the Jews, Mark to the Romans, and Luke to the Greeks. God raised up John to write a Gospel for *everyone*.

During the half century or so since Jesus had ascended, the church had become established and the gospel had spread throughout the known world. A great deal more thinking about the meaning of Jesus' mission and teaching had occurred. In fact, as the first century neared its close, various heresies surrounding the person of Christ began to grow and the purity of the church was threatened. This partly explains why the Holy Spirit inspired and guided John, a close companion of Jesus, to write his Gospel when he did. There was an urgent need for someone who had the authority of an apostle, to speak with clarity and finality about the life and teachings of Jesus. John was the man God chose. His Gospel contains more of Jesus' actual words than any of the other three.

AUTHOR AND DATE

John, the author of the fourth Gospel, is also the writer of four other New Testament books, the three epistles that bear his name and the final book of the New Testament, Revelation. He was the brother of another apostle, James. The two of them worked with their father as fishermen, and were among the first ones chosen by our Lord to be disciples.[93]

John, along with Peter and James, were close friends and eventually became leaders in the Jerusalem church.[94]

---

[93] Mark 1:19–20
[94] Galatians 2:9

John was a man of courage, loyalty, and love. His love for Jesus and people shines forth in this Gospel and also in his three epistles.

He wrote this Gospel near the end of his life, around A.D. 85. This was the first of the five New Testament books that he wrote.

FIRST READERS

It can be safely said, based on its content, that this Gospel was intended for everyone, Jew and Gentile alike. John also seems to especially have in mind unbelievers as he writes.

PURPOSE

John wrote his Gospel with two essential goals in mind: One, to draw unbelievers to a saving faith in Christ, and second, to strengthen believers in their faith.

THEME

Eternal life is only available through Jesus Christ, the only Son of God.

KEY VERSES

"Jesus did many other miraculous signs in the presence of his disciples, which are not recorded in this book. But these are written that you may believe that Jesus is the Christ, the Son of God, and that by believing you may have life in his name" (John 20:30–31).

 First Reading

John's Gospel literally begins *with* "The Gospel." Verses 1:1–18 is the finest short gospel message in the Bible. The actual narrative of John begins immediately *after* this. His Gospel concludes with a statement of intent in 20:30–31, followed by a "postscript" in which he details the reinstatement of Peter as an apostle.

OUTLINE
Life in Jesus, the Son of God

Public ministry   1:1–12:36a
    A. Time of Jesus begins   1:1–4:54
    B. Years in conflict   5:1–12:36a
Private ministry
    A. Day of preparation   12:36b–17:26
    B. Hour of sacrifice   18:1–19:42
    C. Dawn of victory   20:1–21:25

OVERVIEW

John's narrative falls neatly into two parts, each corresponding to a different ministry focus by our Lord: Public and private ministry.

The "hinge" in Jesus' ministry focus is located about midway in the Gospel. It is the last sentence of 12:36, "When he had finished speaking, Jesus left and hid himself from them." Up to this point, Jesus has been sharing the Good News of salvation with everyone, but most have rejected him. Now, looking ahead to the Cross, he begins to give last instructions to his disciples.

1:1 PUBLIC MINISTRY (3 years)		12:36b PRIVATE MINISTRY (few days) 21:25	
introductions to the people	5:1 opposition by the rulers	introductions for the disciples	18:1 crises and triumph

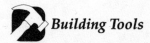 *Building Tools*

IMPORTANT PASSAGES

John's Gospel is so rich in biblical treasure that one could spend a lifetime within its pages. Below are some suggestions for personal study:

1.   JESUS' ENCOUNTERS WITH PEOPLE

    • Nicodemus, an important Jew 3:1–21
    • An unknown Samaritan woman 4:4–38
    • A cowardly apostle 21:15–22

Record your observations and thoughts about these passages on:

> * What Jesus said or didn't say
> * How Jesus treated individuals
> * How Jesus taught

2.   THE UPPER ROOM TEACHING—John 13–17

This material occupies nearly 25 per cent of John's Gospel and appears nowhere else in the Bible. Its value is obvious. From this section, record:

- What is important to Jesus
- What are the "marks" of a true disciple
- What is the primary ministry of the Spirit
- What I can expect in life as a disciple

3.   THE ELEVEN "I AM's" OF JESUS

Look up these and meditate on each one. Record all you can about what each passage reveals about the character of Jesus Christ:

> "I AM . . .
> . . . the Messiah   4:26
> . . . the Bread of Life   6:35
> . . . from above   8:23
> . . . the Eternal One   8:58
> . . . the Light of the World   9:5
> . . . the Door   10:7
> . . . the Son of God   10:36
> . . . the Resurrection and Life   11:25
> . . . the Lord and Master   13:13
> . . . the Way, Truth and Life   14:6
> . . . the True Vine"   15:1

KEY WORDS

believe, love

ACTS
The Beginnings of the Christian Church

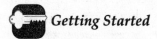 *Getting Started*

The book of Acts serves as a vital link between the four Gospels that precede it and the twenty-two books that follow it. It is primarily a history of the rise and spread of the Christian church throughout the known world. But, it is far from "dry" reading! It is in this book that we find out when and how the Holy Spirit first came to *indwell* God's people; how persecution threatened the church; who the first martyr was; why a militant Pharisee named Saul suddenly became a powerful force *for* the gospel instead of its arch-enemy; and who all the people are to whom the rest of the New Testament is addressed.

A word of caution, however. The book of Acts, because it is historical narrative, should *not* be used as a foundation source for formulating doctrine. It chronicles what happened in the early church, but not the "why." That was left for the rest of the New Testament writers.

RELATION OF ACTS TO THE GOSPELS

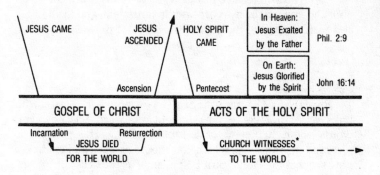

*From Irving L. Jensen, *Jensen's Survey of the New Testament* (Chicago: Moody Press, 1981), 202. Used by permission.

169

AUTHOR AND DATE

Because of the nearly identical content of Luke 1:1–4 and Acts 1:1, we may assume that although unnamed, Acts was written by the author of the third Gospel, Luke.

It is generally accepted that this "sequel" was penned around A.D. 61, near the time of Paul's imprisonment in Rome, described in the closing chapters of Acts.

FIRST READERS

Luke again addressed this book to his friend, Theophilus, but we may be assured his intention is to record an accurate history for *all* to read.

PURPOSE

Luke's purpose in writing this sequel to his Gospel may very well be contained in his opening statement, "In my former book, Theophilus, I wrote about all that *Jesus began to do and to teach* . . ."(1:1, emphasis added). If Luke's Gospel was a record of what Jesus *began* to do and teach, then Acts may correctly be viewed as a record of what Jesus *continued* to do and to teach through his disciples, empowered by the indwelling Holy Spirit.

THEME

Christians are Christ's witnesses of the Good News to the entire world.

KEY VERSE

"But you will receive power when the Holy Spirit comes on you; and you will be my witnesses in Jerusalem, and in all Judea and Samaria, and to the ends of the earth" (1:8).

 First Reading

Read the first paragraph again (1:1–5), noting the person who links Acts with Luke. A new thought appears in Acts, however, words about fulfilment of a promise (1:4). This promise is recorded in John 14:26, which you should go back and read. We now see that the Holy Spirit is spoken of as the "gift."

The last verse of Acts shows something very interesting. Paul speaks openly and freely about his faith in Jesus Christ and delivers the gospel message to all who will gather and listen . . . *while he's imprisoned*! Truly, Jesus' promise in the opening comments of Acts is demonstrated in full glory as the book closes!

OUTLINE
The Beginnings of the Christian Church

Jerusalem
    A. The church is born   1:1–2:47
    B. The church grows through testing   3:1–8:1a
Judea and Samaria
    A. The church is scattered   8:1b–9:31
    B. The church embraces the Gentiles   9:32–12:25
Every part of the world
    A. The church extends overseas   13:1–21:17
    B. The church's leader on trial   21:18–28:31

OVERVIEW

ACTS: BEGINNINGS OF THE CHRISTIAN CHURCH

1:1 JERUSALEM	8:1b JUDEA and SAMARIA	13:1 EVERY PART OF THE WORLD 28:31
CHURCH BORN AND TESTED	CHURCH SCATTERED	CHURCH EXTENDED
JEWISH PERIOD	TRANSITION	UNVERSAL GOSPEL

A good place to begin for getting an overview of the whole book of Acts is the key verse: ". . .you will be my witnesses in Jerusalem, and in all Judea and Samaria, and to the ends of the earth"(1:8b). If you examine the maps at the back of this book, you will see immediately that Jesus' statement involved a progression *out* from Jerusalem, like a series of concentric circles. Following the story through the book of Acts, you will discover that this is exactly what happened, and how it happened.

There were also two other progressions during these years:

(1) The church was *born and grew* through testing(1:1–8:1a); it was *scattered* by persecutions (8:1b–12:25); and it *spread* to the ends of the earth through missions (13:1–28:31).

(2) Nearly all the believers in the early churches were *Jews*

(1:1–8:1a); the apostles soon began to preach that the Good News was also for *Gentiles* (8:1b–12:25); and eventually the church's message was recognized as a universal gospel—for *everyone* (13:1–28:31).

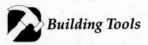 *Building Tools*

IMPORTANT PASSAGES

With the overview in mind, below are some sections of the book of Acts rich for mining biblical principles. After you've selected the sections you wish to study further, read the section over a number of times, paying special attention to:

- The relationships between believers and non-believers
- The methods of ministry
- The personal character of the key figures
- The specifics of the *faith* of the key figures

IMPORTANT SECTIONS IN THE BOOK OF ACTS

The "birth" of the church	2:10–47
Fellowship in the early church	4:23–37
The life and death of Stephen	6:1–8:1a
The conversion of Saul of Tarsus	9:1–19a
The church is extended to the Gentiles	9:32–12:25
Paul the missionary	13:1–21:17
Paul the prisoner	21:18–28:31

KEY WORDS

witness, preach, boldly

ROMANS
God's Salvation for Sinners

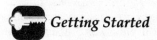 **Getting Started**

One of the best ways to saturate the drinking water of a city with any substance is to introduce it at the source, the spring from which it all flows. God used a similar method in spreading the gospel. The city of Rome was the most important city in the world during the first century. By planting a vibrant church in that city, God would enable the gospel to spread quickly throughout the world. The phrase, "All roads lead to Rome" was true!

It is to a church in this city that the book of Romans is addressed. Romans contains the most thorough and detailed explanation of what it means to become and live as a Christian. It was imperative that such an influential city should have a clear presentation of the truth. The book of Romans was that presentation.

AUTHOR AND DATE

The opening verse leaves no doubt as to who the author of this great letter is. Paul clearly states that it is he that writes, and also lays claim to being "called to be an apostle and set apart for the gospel of God . . . "(1:1). We learned of the conversion of this famous Jew in the book of Acts.

Paul was born of Jewish parents, probably very close to the time of Christ's birth. He was raised in a strict sect known as the Pharisees, and quickly became a leader of zealous Jews who wanted to exterminate Christianity.[95] In fact, his conversion to Christianity occurred while en route to imprison Christians! We know from the letter that Paul had never personally visited the Roman church,[96] although we can also surmise from this letter that he was planning to make such a trip soon.[97]

---

[95] Acts 26:4-11
[96] see 1:13 and 15:28
[97] see 1:10-15 and 15:22-29

Paul wrote this letter near the end of his third missionary journey, from the city of Corinth in Greece,[98] which would have been around A.D. 56.

FIRST READERS

There was apparently a strong church in the city because Paul specifically addresses his letter to them. However, because we know that Paul had never visited the city, he was not the church's founder. The fellowship in Rome was mixed, consisting of converted Jews and Gentiles, meeting in various homes and other places. The population of Rome at this time was probably close to one million. Also, the Roman emperors were considered gods by many of the citizens, which would make the Christians "stand out." Being a Christian in Rome would not have been easy!

PURPOSE

Paul's letter is intended to instruct, encourage, and strengthen the church in this influential city in the basic truths of the gospel.

THEME

The righteousness of God is given to the sinner who believes in Jesus Christ.

KEY VERSES

"I am not ashamed of the gospel, because it is the power of God for the salvation of everyone who believes: first for the Jew, then for the Gentile. For in the gospel a righteousness from God is revealed, a righteousness that is by faith from first to last" (1:16–17a).

 First Reading

The first seventeen verses of the book, called a *prologue*, are Paul's greeting and introduction to the whole book (1:1–17). Read this warm *prologue* now. Then go to the end of the book and read the *epilogue*, which is made up of personal messages also. Only in the *epilogue*, Paul refers to specific people. One can almost feel the

---

[98]Acts 18:23-21:17; also the name, "Gaius" appears both in Romans 16:23 and 1 Corinthians 1:14

excitement and enthusiasm in Paul's heart as he wrote!

In comparing the way the book begins and ends, we get a sense of victory and fulfilment. For example, near the beginning Paul wrote a warm note of gratitude: "I thank my God through Jesus Christ for all of you"(1:8), and his last line is one of loud praise: "To the only wise God be glory for ever through Jesus Christ!" (16:27). This is truly a book of triumphant proclamation.

OUTLINE
God's Salvation for Sinners

    Prologue   1:1–17
    Doctrine   1:18–11:36
        A. God's holiness in condemning sin   1:18–3:20
        B. God's grace in making sinners "right"   3:21–5:21
        C. God's power in making believers holy   6:1–8:39
        D. God's design in saving Jew and Gentile
           9:1–11:36
    Practice   12:1–15:13
        A. The Christian servant   12:1–21
        B. The Christian citizen   13:1–14
        C. The Christian brother   14:1–15:13
    Epilogue   15:14–16:27

OVERVIEW

ROMANS: GOD'S SALVATION FOR SINNERS

PROLOGUE 1:1-17	DOCTRINAL			"Amen"	"So"	PRACTICAL	EPILOGUE 15:14 - 16:27
	1:18 SIN	3:21 SALVATION	6:1 SANCTI-FICATION	9:1 SOVEREIGNTY		12:1 SERVICE 15:13	
	GOD'S HOLINESS	GOD'S GRACE	GOD'S POWER	GOD'S SOVEREIGNTY		GOD'S GLORY	

The book of Romans, like most of Paul's letters, is divided into two major sections: doctrine (right teaching) and application (right living). In this particular book, the divisions are 1:18–11:36 and 12:1–15:13 respectively. It is perhaps noteworthy that the doctrinal section *ends* with the word "Amen!" and the application section *begins* with the word "therefore." Within these two major divisions are five minor sections, each focusing on a different aspect of the theme—salvation.

• *The need of salvation* (1:18–3:20). In this section, Paul in perhaps his most masterful attempt, demonstrates that there is *no one* who is free from the sting and guilt of sin.

• *The way of salvation* (3:21–5:21). Here Paul demonstrates the central theme of salvation by faith, even reaching back into the history of the Jews to show that salvation by faith is not some "new" idea with God.

• *The life of salvation* (6:1–8:39). Paul addresses the Christian's battle with sin and the flesh and explains the joyous deliverance through life in the Spirit. This section ends with what is perhaps the most majestic presentation on the security of the believer in Christ in the entire Bible.

• *The scope of salvation* (9:1–11:36). In these difficult passages, Paul lays bare God's plan for humanity. He addresses the purposes for national Israel and the privilege extended to the Gentiles.

• *The service of salvation* (12:1–15:13). Here Paul expounds and explains the practical outworkings of the gospel in the lives of those touched by it. He discusses spiritual gifts, citizenship and its responsibilities, and how to get along with believers who share different convictions on "grey issues".

 *Building Tools*

IMPORTANT PASSAGES

When one examines the main passages of the book of Romans, it explains why one Bible student exclaimed, "A thorough study of this epistle is really a theological education in itself!" Below are some passages deserving of careful examination.

- The whole world condemned   1:18–3:20
- Justification (making "right" with God)   3:21–5:21
- Sanctification (making "holy" like Christ)   6:1–8:39
- Israel (past) chapter 9; (present) chapter 10; (future) chapter 11
- Christian conduct   12:1–15:13

KEY WORDS

sin, righteousness, faith, Spirit

1 CORINTHIANS
Problems of a Local Church

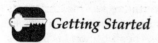 *Getting Started*

Corinth was the capital of the Roman province of Achaia, which today is the southern half of Greece. It was the second largest city in Achaia. However, it was the number one city for commerce, and therefore it was the *richest*. The temple of Aphrodite, the Greek goddess of love, was in Corinth, along with its one thousand sacred prostitutes. The sexual immorality of Corinth was so internationally well-known that there actually was a derogatory word used in Paul's day that meant to "live like a Corinthian"!

Paul had "planted" this church in the business centre of Greece while on his second missionary journey.[99] The new converts from that visit started a local church. Then, about five years later, Paul wrote this letter in an attempt to straighten out the difficulties that had developed.

The church in Corinth was riddled with problems, especially in their relationships with one another. There were divisions over leadership, incest, marital problems, believers suing each other, impropriety during the Lord's Supper, and many more. It was a pastor's worst nightmare.

It was into this spiritual arena that Paul addressed this letter. He wrote from a broken heart, but with the faith and confidence that they would repent and God would heal their church.

AUTHOR AND DATE

Once again, Paul identifies himself as the author of this letter (1:1). Unlike the letter to the Romans, Paul was familiar both with the city and its people. He had been there himself.

Paul wrote 1 Corinthians while on his third missionary journey, from the city of Ephesus[100] around A.D. 55. This is the first of

[99] Acts 17:15-18:18
[100] 1 Corinthians 16:8

three epistles Paul wrote while on this journey. The other two are Romans and 2 Corinthians.

FIRST READERS

The Christians in Corinth were "young" in the Lord, and had been converted out of paganism. Because of the metropolitan nature of Corinth, the believers were undoubtedly a mixed group— Jewish converts, pagans who were former devotees of Aphrodite, and probably some wealthy upper-class Greeks.

Paul addressed them as "the church of God in Corinth, to those sanctified in Christ Jesus"(1:2). Their position in Christ of *holiness* is because they have believed the Good News of salvation and received the righteousness described in Romans. But they are presently guilty of sins that are tearing apart the church.

PURPOSE

The obvious purposes of this letter are:
- to correct false doctrine
- to help the believers see their sins and weaknesses
- to encourage them in how to have a healthy, maturing Christian life

THEME

Jesus Christ and the indwelling Holy Spirit answer all the spiritual problems of Christians and the local churches where they worship and fellowship.

KEY VERSES

"But thanks be to God! He gives us the victory through our Lord Jesus Christ. Therefore, my dear brothers, stand firm. Let nothing move you. Always give yourselves fully to the work of the Lord, because you know that your labour in the Lord is not in vain"(15:57–58).

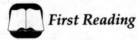 *First Reading*

Reading the introduction to the letter (1:1–9), we see Paul extolling the goodness of God and affirming his confidence in God's work in their lives. He ends the letter (chapter 16) on a positive note, too. Yet, in between these two encouragements are some severe chastisements and rebukes. Paul's approach should be a lesson to us today. When it becomes necessary to deal with sin in another's life, "sandwiching" it between encouragement and confidence in God's grace is a good idea!

OUTLINE
Problems of a Local Church

Introduction   1:1–9
Bad reports   1:10–6:20
    A. Divisions   1:10–4:23
    B. Disorders   5:1–6:20
Answering questions   7:1–15:58
    A. Personal problems   7:1–11:1
    B. Public worship problems   11:2–14:40
    C. Questions about the resurrection   15:1–58
Conclusion   16:1–24

OVERVIEW

1 CORINTHIANS: PROBLEMS OF A LOCAL CHURCH

INTRODUCTION 1:1-9	ACKNOWLEDGING REPORTS		ANSWERING INQUIRIES			CONCLUSION 16:1-24
	problems of the congregation		personal problems	worship service problems		
	DISUNITY	DEPRAVITIES	MARRIAGE	CHRISTIAN LIBERTY	ORDER, SPIRITUAL GIFTS, AND RESURRECTION	
	1:10	5:1	7:1	8:1	11:2 15:58	

The letter of 1 Corinthians is actually *Paul's response to a letter from them* in which they had asked some very specific questions regarding personal and corporate issues.[101] He also writes as a result of hearing reports about the church's problems. From this we can conclude that there are two main sections to the letter: bad reports (1:10–6:20) and answering questions (7:1–15:58). As you read, keep these two divisions in mind. It is exciting to see that there are no problems in 1 Corinthians without answers, which makes the book so valuable to us today. The resurrected Christ and the indwelling Holy Spirit provide believers with sufficient

[101] In 7:1 Paul says, "Now, for the matters you wrote about . . ."

answers. Some of the problems that the reports and the questions centred around were:

•*Not getting along together* (1:10–4:23). "I beg that all of you agree with one another." Paul seeks to help them understand the centrality of Christ rather than allegiance to specific leaders, etc.

•*Disorders* (5:1–6:20). Paul writes about carelessness(5:1–13); lawsuits (6:1–11); and immorality (6:12–20).

•*Marriage* (7:1–40). Paul answers some perplexing questions about marriage, widows, being single and sexual sin.

•*Christian freedom* (8:1–11:1). We learn from these passages how to apply Christian principles to questionable practices, "grey areas," today.

•*Public worship* (11:2–14:40). The place of women and men in worship (11:2–16); the Lord's Supper (11:17–34); and spiritual gifts (12:1–14:40).

•*The resurrection body* (15:1–58). This is the key chapter of 1 Corinthians. The people had two questions about the resurrection, and Paul answers both: "Will people be raised from the dead?"(15:12); and "What kind of body will they have?" (15:35).

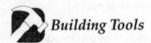 *Building Tools*

IMPORTANT PASSAGES

First Corinthians contains a great deal of doctrine as well as ample practical instruction for holy living. Below are a few fragments of the book in which you will discover truths that enlighten and encourage as much today as they did in the first century. As you select some for study, pay special attention to:

- Practical suggestions for getting along with others
- Solid biblical truth to encourage and sustain
- Reasons to hope in the present

1 Corinthians 15—the "resurrection" chapter
1 Corinthians 13—the "love" chapter
1 Corinthians 10—the "warning" chapter
1 Corinthians 2—the "wisdom" chapter

KEY WORDS

wisdom, resurrection, cross, body(man's), body of Christ, "in Christ Jesus"

2 CORINTHIANS
Gospel Ministry and God's Gifts

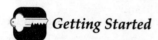 *Getting Started*

This letter is addressed to the same church as 1 Corinthians. It too, has to do with meeting problems in the local church. Apparently, some of the Christians there began seriously to doubt Paul's authority as an apostle of Christ. Between his first letter and this one, Paul's travelling companion, Titus, made a visit to Corinth to see how they were doing after Paul's first letter.[102] The report that Titus brings back to Paul is somewhat "bittersweet." There has been repentance and growth in many areas, but there is also a group within the church that does not respect Paul. This letter is Paul's *response* to the report of Titus.

AUTHOR AND DATE

Paul states his authorship in the opening verse. This time, Timothy is with him as he writes. It is obvious from the letter itself that Paul is in Macedonia (just north of Greece) on his third missionary journey, and on his way to Corinth for a visit. The date is about one year after 1 Corinthians, A.D. 56.

FIRST READERS

Paul wrote this letter to the identical group of his previous letter. They still needed spiritual help, which Paul offered through this "follow-up" letter and another personal visit.[103] It is remarkable that Paul is able to maintain such an attitude of service and love towards a church that has presented such difficult challenges every step of the way. There is a great deal for us to learn from the faithful, arduous efforts of this man of God.

---

[102] see 2 Corinthians 2:12 and 7:5-16
[103] 12:14; 13:1

PURPOSE

The primary reasons Paul wrote this second letter were to encourage the people for their repentance and growth, and to defend himself because of criticism by certain people in the church.[104] A secondary reason was to give further instruction about an offering for the poor believers in Jerusalem for whom Paul was responsible.[105]

THEME

God gave us *all* this work—to tell everyone that Jesus Christ is Lord (4:1,5).

KEY VERSES

"We are therefore Christ's ambassadors, as though God were making his appeal through us. We implore you on Christ's behalf: Be reconciled to God. God made him who had no sin to be sin for us, so that in him we might become the righteousness of God" (5:20–21).

 First Reading

When we compare the beginning and end of this letter, we discover a *thankful* apostle as the book opens,[106] and a gracious *friend* as the book closes.[107] Paul's second letter to the Corinthian church is an inspiration for us to learn how a person active in the ministry can handle the pressure and pain that accompanies it.

OUTLINE
Gospel Ministry and God's Gifts

    Greeting   1:1–2
        A. Sketch of Paul's ministry   1:3–7:16
        B. Appeal about giving   8:1–9:15
        C. Defence of Paul's ministry   10:1–13:10
    Farewell   13:11–14

---

[104] see 10:10 and 13:3
[105] 9:1-5; see also 1 Corinthians 16:3
[106] 1:1-11
[107] 13:5-14

OVERVIEW

2 CORINTHIANS: PAUL'S MINISTRY AND GOD'S GIFTS

SALUTATION 1:1-2	SKETCH OF PAUL'S MINISTRY	APPEAL FOR GIVING	DEFENCE OF PAUL'S MINISTRY	CONCLUSION 13:11-14
	1:3	8:1	10:1 · · · · · · · · · · 13:10	

Second Corinthians consists of three main parts. Using the outline and diagram above, read them one section at a time. You will find the following subdivisions helpful in your reading:

A Sketch of Paul's Ministry 1:3–7:16
Good relations with fellow Christians (1:3–2:13). After the opening greeting, Paul cleared up false reports about his changed plans to visit Corinth. He wanted people to know how much he loved them *and* that his word could be trusted.

Ministry of the gospel (2:14–7:3). Paul's subjects in this section are the gospel message itself, the fact that he keeps on preaching it even when weary, and the joy he experiences being sent to speak for Christ.

Joy in sorrow (7:4–16). "I am greatly encouraged; in all our troubles my joy knows no bounds"(7:4). It is interesting in this section to see just what it is that produces such joy in this weary apostle—it is the Corinthians and their response to God!

Appeal for Giving 8:1–9:15
This section contains the most detailed account in the New Testament on the Christian's freedom and responsibility in giving to God. It ends with a reminder of the proper motivation in giving: "Thanks be to God for his indescribable gift!"

Paul's Defence of His Ministry 10:1–13:10
This section is one of the most moving portions of Paul's writings, providing us with a rare "behind the scenes" look at this man of God. Paul speaks of his credentials, his work, his pain, and his authority. We learn more about Paul's personal life from his own mouth in this section than perhaps anywhere else in the New Testament. His defence was aimed at false apostles and the Corinthian believers whom they led astray from the truth as revealed to them by Paul. The Christian world of the first century

wanted to know: "Who are the *real* emissaries of Christ?" Paul's second Corinthian letter gives an answer for all time to people everywhere.

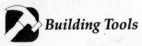 *Building Tools*

IMPORTANT PASSAGES

Because of the intensely personal nature of this letter, it is not as tightly organized as Paul's other writings. Therefore, a thematic approach to studying it is best. Below are a few themes that will provide rich insight into your own relationship with God. As you read and take notes, be sensitive for thoughts and principles regarding:

- The ministry: its joys and sorrows
- Life: its joys and sorrows (i.e., proper expectations)

How God works *in* those who minister   chapter 4
Life from "Paul's side of the fence"   6:3–10; 11:16–33
Giving God's way   chapters 8–9

KEY WORDS

sorrow, glory, comfort

GALATIANS
Set Free in Christ

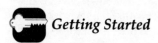 **Getting Started**

The book of Galatians, earliest of thirteen New Testament letters written by the apostle Paul, is easier to understand when we discover *why* it was written. On his first missionary journey, Paul and his companions preached the gospel in cities in the southern region of a province known as Galatia, in Asia Minor.[108] It included such cities as Antioch, Iconium, Lystra and Derbe (see map on page 302). This region is now known as Turkey. They had a very fruitful ministry in this region and many churches were begun.

After Paul and his helpers had left the area, some other teachers arrived and told these relatively new Christians that Paul had not given them the "whole gospel"—there was more to being a Christian than mere faith. In particular, they told the Galatian believers that they needed to also observe many of the Jewish customs and ceremonies, especially circumcision. In short, they told them that they could not be genuine believers if they did not first become practising Jews!

AUTHOR AND DATE

Paul clearly states that he is the author of this letter, and also indicates that there are a number of "brothers" in the Lord with him. It is likely that Paul wrote this letter *before* the Jerusalem Council described in Acts 15, which would make it some time in A.D. 48.

FIRST READERS

Galatians is one of the few letters written by Paul to a *province* rather than an individual person or city. Paul clearly wrote to the

---

[108] Acts 13:1-14:28

"churches" in Galatia, indicating that it was meant for many different readers.

PURPOSE

One of the central issues the letter to the Galatians sought to address was the same as that discussed at the Jerusalem Council, namely, "What is the responsibility of Gentile converts to Christianity in relation to the Jewish laws and customs? Do they have to go through all the same requirements that the Jews had to (as Jews), before *they* became believers?" It is difficult for us, nearly twenty centuries later, to appreciate the incredible bias many of the Jews of Paul's day had in their thinking. Judaism had been around for nearly two thousand years. Making a complete "switch" to a religion that did not have the customs, rituals, feasts, and all that went with them, was not an easy transition for the Jewish Christians. Those who wanted to maintain the link with the past were known as Judaizers. Had they won this debate, Christianity's unique message of salvation would more than likely have been silenced. Another faction in the Galatian churches had the opposite opinion: "If Christ has set us free, then we can live as we please!" Paul's response to both of these errors lies somewhere between the two extremes.

THEME

Only faith can save us from slavery to the law. We are to live our Christian lives by following God's Spirit in freedom, not the law in bondage.

KEY VERSE

"After beginning with the Spirit, are you now trying to attain your goal by human effort?" (3:3)

 First Reading

We can see from a casual glance at the opening and closing comments of this letter[109] that it does not have the warm and personal tone that characterizes most of Paul's writings. It is clear

---

[109]See 1:1-5, where Paul launches right into a rather stinging question after a brief greeting, and 6:11-18 where he takes a hard "shot" at the Judaizers' attempts to turn the Galatians back to slavery to the Jewish law.

that he is writing to correct error, and it is error that he is not too pleased with!

OUTLINE
Set Free in Christ

Introduction   1:1–5
   A. The source of the gospel   1:6–2:21
   B. The defence of the gospel   3:1–5:1
   C. The application of the gospel   5:2–6:10
Conclusion   6:11–18

OVERVIEW

	PERSONAL TESTIMONY	TEACHING THE TRUTH	LIVING THE TRUTH	
SALUTATION 1:1-5	GOOD NEWS	LAW	SPIRIT	**CONCLUSION 6:11-18**
	The Good News I Preach Is From God	The Good News Is Better Than the Law	God's Spirit Gives Freedom	
	1:6	3:1	5:2	

Before reading the letter, we should have a clear picture of the whole. While reading this letter, look for the following divisions of thought:

• *The gospel* (1:6–2:21). In this section, Paul outlines his own relationship to the gospel, how he received it, and more importantly the fact that there are "other" Gospels that are false.
• *The Law* (3:1-5:1). In this section, Paul labours over the purpose of the law and its inadequacies in regard to salvation.
• *The Spirit* (5:2–6:10). In this final section, Paul discusses the real definition of "freedom in Christ," which is neither slavery to law nor irresponsible looseness. This section is one of the "Golden Sections" of Scripture because of its clarity and loftiness in regard to true spirituality.

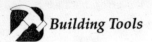 *Building Tools*

IMPORTANT PASSAGES

Below are three sections from Galatians worth investigating. Beneath each section are some suggestions on what to look for:

The Christian's liberty—5:1–18
- What does true "freedom" consist of?
- What does it *not* consist of?
- Using Paul's definitions, are *you* free?

The flesh—5:19–21; 6:7–8
- Which items in this list were you surprised to see?
- Which items are in *your* life right now?

The Spirit-controlled life—5:22–26; 6:1–10
- Which items listed here are lacking in your life?
- How do you see Jesus demonstrating these qualities?

KEY WORDS

In this letter, there are three key words and they conveniently correspond to the three main sections of Galatians. They are:

- "gospel" 15 times in the first section
- "Law"   29 times in the second section
- "Spirit" 10 times in the last section

Follow these words through their respective sections, taking note of any insights you discover. Be especially alert for how they each are used to accomplish Paul's goal.

EPHESIANS
Christ and the Church

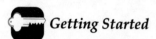

Getting Started

When we want to think about the truths of who Christ is and what he did, Ephesians is the book to read. It is Paul's masterpiece, sometimes called the "Grand Canyon" of Scripture, because its truths are so deep and wide, yet beautiful to behold.

Paul's first contact with the Christians at Ephesus was a very brief visit to their Jewish synagogue, on his second missionary journey in A.D. 52.[110] On his third journey, he taught the people of that area for three years.[111] Then, soon after returning to Jerusalem, the apostle was arrested and falsely accused as a troublemaker.[112] He was sent to Rome for a fair trial. During this imprisonment in Rome, he wrote four letters. Ephesians is the longest and most grand of the four.

AUTHOR AND DATE

From the internal evidence, it is clear that Paul wrote this letter around A.D. 61–62 from Rome. It was brought to the first readers by a young man named Tychicus, who also carried Paul's letters to the Colossians and the slave owner Philemon.[113]

FIRST READERS

This letter was probably a "circular" letter. That is, it was passed from one church to another after it was read. Ephesus was a large coastal city on the coast of Asia (see map on page 302) about four hundred miles west of Galatia. The church of Ephesus was probably the first and last church to read the letter in its circula-

---

[110] see Acts 18:19-21
[111] A.D. 52-54; see also Acts 18:23-21:16
[112] Acts 24:15
[113] see Ephesians 6:21; Colossians 4:7

tion. The first readers of Ephesians were a mixture of Jews and Gentiles who had become Christians during Paul's earlier visits.

PURPOSE

Paul had two main purposes in writing, each expressed by a prayer recorded in the letter (paraphrased):

"I pray that you may come to know your resources in Christ"(chapters 1–3).
"I pray that you may live consistent with your faith in Christ"(chapters 4–6).

He also sought to convince them of the unity of Jew and Gentile "in Christ."

THEME

Christians' lives should show their faith in Christ, because of their never ending resources in Christ and the powerful work of God in their lives.

KEY VERSES

"[God seated Christ] far above all rule and authority, power and dominion, and every title that can be given, not only in the present age but also in the one to come. And God placed all things under his feet and appointed him to be head over everything for the church," (Ephesians 1:21b–22).

 First Reading

Because this is a lengthy letter, you may want to read the introduction (1:1–2), scan the segment titles (in your Bible), and read the conclusion (6:21–24) before you read it more thoughtfully.

OUTLINE
Christ and the Church

Introduction   1:1–2
    A. Our heritage in Christ   1:3–3:21
        1. Spiritual blessings in Christ   1:3–14
        2. Prayer for spiritual wisdom   1:15–23

OVERVIEW

In looking for the book's structure, or how Paul put it together, we can pick up a clue at the end of chapter 3: the last word is "Amen," and the last verse (3:21) is a doxology of praise to God. The tiny word "Amen" divides the book into two parts: the *work* of God (1:3–3:21) and the *walk* of the believer (4:1–6:20).

SALUTATION 1:1-2	WORK OF GOD			WALK OF THE CHRISTIAN		CONCLUSION 6:21-24
	1:3	2:1	3:1	4:1	6:10	
	Blessings "in Christ"	Experience of Salvation	Growing in Knowledge and Strength	Christian Behaviour	Christian Armour	
	WE IN CHRIST			CHRIST IN US		

• *Blessings in Christ* (1:3–23). See how often the words "in Christ" appear in this section. This is an important section in this letter, and could easily be titled, "Spiritual Blessings in Christ." The prayers of 1:15–23 and 3:14–21 in this section are among the most grand and richest in all of God's Word.

• *Experiences of salvation* (2:1–22). Here Paul discusses what has happened to them as individuals in coming to Christ, and the practical outworking of that corporately, especially as it relates to Jews and Gentiles together.

• *Growing in knowledge and strength* (3:1–20). Paul begins this section telling of his call from God to be an apostle to the Gentiles, and concludes it by telling them precisely what he is praying for *their* lives.

• *Christian behaviour* (4:1-6:9). Paul describes in great detail what type of conduct should characterize those who have been "made alive" in Christ. He deals with every type of relationship they would encounter.

• *Christian armour* (6:10-20). In this last section, Paul provides us with the most detailed account in the New Testament of the nature of the Christian's warfare with Satan and the means of withstanding it.

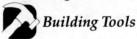 *Building Tools*

IMPORTANT PASSAGES

The letter to the Ephesians is one of the richest storehouses of doctrinal and practical truth we have. Below are just a few of the great themes it contains, for your personal study.

1. MY POSITION IN CHRIST 1:3–2:10
   • List the "riches" that are yours as a Christian.
   • Write out what life would be like *without* them.
   • Take some time and thank God for them, one by one.
2. THE PRAYERS OF PAUL 1:15–23; 3:14–21
   • Write out what Paul wants God to do in their lives.
   • Select one or two items in his list for further study.
   • Which items could you pray for yourself? for others?
3. THE CHRISTIAN'S TONGUE 4:29–5:4
   • How does Paul say you should talk?
   • What are areas needing attention in *your* life?
4. THE CHRISTIAN HOME 5:21–6:4
   • Why is verse 21 so important?
   • Write out specific ways *you* can be faithful to the instruction given in these verses for you.
   • What can you pray for yourself and others from the truths of these verses?
5. THE ARMOUR OF GOD 6:10-18
   • Write out what each piece of armour is and why you think it is important.
   • Which pieces are lacking from your arsenal?

KEY WORDS

church, "in Christ," power, riches

PHILIPPIANS
Life in Christ

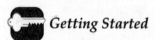 *Getting Started*

Philippi is often called the birthplace of European Christianity, because the book of Acts records that the first believer in Europe was saved here.[114] This happened around A.D. 50, on Paul's second missionary journey.[115] Paul gained many new friends in the Macedonian city of Philippi (see map on page 302) in northern Greece on his first missionary journey, and they continued to be a source of joy in the years that followed.[116] Paul had also suffered persecution in Philippi[117] which may account partly for the *depth* of friendship. Suffering often creates a bond that abundance cannot create.

After his first visit at Philippi, Paul's friend Luke remained behind to teach the new believers and help the start a church. By the time Paul writes them this letter from the prison at Rome, six years later, the church was a growing fellowship.

Philippians is the most joyful of all Paul's writings. There is less correction and more praise in its pages than any other New Testament book he wrote. Down through the ages Philippians has helped renew the spiritual life of many Christians.

AUTHOR AND DATE

Paul states himself clearly as the·writer of this letter in the opening verse. Timothy was apparently with him in Rome when it was written. Paul was under "house arrest" at this time, which meant he was still incarcerated, but under minimum security. Philippians was written some time between A.D. 61–62.

---

[114] Acts 16:14–15
[115] Acts 16:12-40
[116] see Philippians 1:3-8
[117] see 1 Thessalonians 2:2

FIRST READERS

The church in Philippi was somewhat different in makeup from the other churches Paul had founded. It had very few, if any, Jews. We know that the Jewish population of the city was small because Paul could not find a synagogue there when he first visited on his second missionary journey.[118] Philippi was a Roman colony and the population of Philippi consisted of a large number of retired Roman soldiers. This helps us appreciate the horror that the Philippian jailor felt when he discovered that he had imprisoned a Roman citizen (Paul) without a just cause![119]

PURPOSE

Some of the obvious reasons Paul wrote this letter are *personal*. He wanted to thank them for the generous gift they had sent, explain why he was sending Epaphroditus back to them, and tell them of his plans to send Timothy to them shortly. Throughout the letter Paul overflows with thankfulness for the friendship he enjoyed with this church. The other reason he wrote was *practical*. It seems that there was a problem among them with rivalry and selfish competition. Paul addresses this issue head-on, using Jesus as an example of humility and generosity in one of the most stirring passages in the New Testament.[120]

THEME

The secret of true joy for the believer is living in Christ.

KEY VERSE

"For to me, to live is Christ and to die is gain" (1:21).

 First Reading

This letter opens and closes with an attitude of thanksgiving and joy. Paul's first comments to them are words we all long to hear, "I thank my God every time I remember you" (1:3). He closes the letter in a similar way, reminding them of their generosity to him and the unique place they hold in his heart as a result (4:14–20).

---

[118] see Acts 16:12-16. The "place of prayer" spoken of here indicates that there was no formal synagogue for the Jews living in Philippi.
[119] see Acts 16:22-39
[120] Philippians 2:1-11

OUTLINE
Life in Christ

OVERVIEW

Because of the intensely personal nature of Philippians, it is hard to find any obvious outline of ideas. Below is a visual representation of the book's general divisions:

TESTIMONY	EXAMPLES		TEACHING
Present Attitudes ➡	Aims and Desires	⬅	Present Sufficiency
CHRIST OUR LIFE	CHRIST OUR EXAMPLE	CHRIST OUR GOAL	CHRIST OUR SUPPLY
1:1	1:27	3:1	4:2

As you read the following sections, keep in mind the primary theme of Philippians: "Life in Christ."

• *Christ our Life* (1:1–26). The reason Paul prays for his friends, loves them dearly, and handles troubles without giving up the Lord's work, is Christ.

• *Christ our Example* (1:27–2:30). A great section when one considers that the goal of God for each of our lives is to make us like Jesus Christ. Here, Christ the obedient servant is held forth as our example.

• *Christ our Goal* (3:1–4:1). Chapter 3 is the mountain peak of Philippians. Here Paul details just what it is that keeps him going forward in the Christian experience. Paul's goal should be ours as well.

• *Christ our Supply* (4:2–23). Paul holds Jesus himself up as the source of our power, joy and peace.

 *Building Tools*

IMPORTANT PASSAGES

Below are several suggestions for further study from the pages of this incredible letter. As you study them, use the following questions as "springboards" for mental discussion:

- How are these characteristics reflected in Jesus' life?
- How are these characteristics reflected in *my* life?
- Why is God so concerned about these qualities?
- How can I build these qualities into my life?

PASSAGE	THEME
2:1–4	The proper relationships among Christians
2:5–11	The humility of Christ
2:12–18	The proper attitude for the Christian
3:7–16	The proper priority for the Christian
4:8–9	The proper mind-set for the Christian

KEY WORDS

Joy, "in Christ," love

THE THREE LETTERS COMPARED

Now that we've finished reading and studying Galatians, Ephesians and Philippians, all written by Paul, it would be helpful to compare the three letters for style, subject matter, purpose, and overall tone.

GALATIANS, EPHESIANS, and PHILIPPIANS COMPARED

	GALATIANS	EPHESIANS	PHILIPPIANS
Style	mainly logic and argument	doctrine and exhortation	information and consolation
A Main Subject	Salvation	Christ the Saviour	Life of Joy
Purpose	correction	edification	inspiration
Tone	sharp, rebuking	calm, victorious	tender, joyful

COLOSSIANS
Christ Is *All and* In *All*

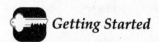 *Getting Started*

False religious groups called cults are a constant threat to Christians. But, they are not a *recent* menace. They were just as rampant in Paul's day as they are in ours! Twisting and denying the truth, tempting people away from the truth of God's Word, various organized heresies were infiltrating the first century church. Colossians is an excellent book to read for that reason alone. It shows how the apostle Paul handled the false teachings of the cults of his day.

All of Paul's letters from prison, including this one, give much attention to the person and work of Jesus Christ. The differences in the letters are in their purposes. For example, in Ephesians (which is *very* similar in content to Colossians), Paul focused on *Christ and the church*. In Colossians, his focus was larger, he wrote about *Christ and the universe*![121] In Ephesians, the emphasis was on the church, the body of Christ. In Colossians it is more on Christ, the Head of the church.

AUTHOR AND DATE

Once again, Paul claims authorship and states that Timothy is present with him at its composition. This shouldn't surprise us though, because we have already established that Philippians, Ephesians and Colossians were all written at about the same time from the same place—house arrest in Rome. The date of this "prison epistle" is around A.D. 61.

FIRST READERS

Paul sent the letter to the church at Colossae (1:2) and asked them to share it with the church in neighbouring Laodicea. The city

---

[121] Note the phrase, ". . . things in heaven and on earth"(1:16).

of Colossae was located on the Lycus River on the great Ephesian Highway about one hundred miles east of the city of Ephesus (see the map on page 302). Because we know that Paul had never visited this city,[122] it is likely that the Colossian church sprung up as result of his extended ministry in Ephesus when, according to Luke, "...all the Jews and Greeks who lived in the province of Asia heard the word of the Lord"(Acts 19:10). Epaphras (1:7) and Archippus (4:17), two leaders in the Colossians church were perhaps among the first ones converted.

PURPOSE

This letter is clearly a *defence* of Christianity in the face of false doctrine that was threatening the Colossian church and those around it. Among the heresies taking root were these:

(1) Jewish religious requirements such as circumcision,[123] rules to follow,[124] and foods and religious holidays[125]
(2) An emphasis on severe self-denial as a sign of spirituality[126]
(3) The worship of angels[127]
(4) An exaggeration, almost worship, of knowledge[128]

Paul virtually dismantles these heresies by presenting the truth about who Jesus Christ is and what he has done for us.

THEME

Christ is supreme (3:11).

KEY VERSES

"All things were created by him and for him. He is before all things, and in him all things hold together"(1:16b–17).

---

[122] see 2:1
[123] 2:11; 3:11
[124] 2:14
[125] 2:16
[126] 2:16, 20-23
[127] 2:18
[128] 2:8

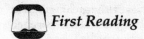

First Reading

Paul opens and closes this letter talking about prayer. He tells the Colossians at the very beginning how much he prays for *them* (1:3, 9–14). He closes the book admonishing *them* to pray for themselves and him. In a book that deals with the nature and effects of false teaching, prayer is seen as a vital weapon in the battle!

OUTLINE

Christ *Is* All and *In* All

> Introduction   1:1–2
> > A. Christian thanksgiving   1:3–12
> > B. True belief   1:13–2:5
> > C. False beliefs   2:6–23
> > D. Christian living   3:1–4:6
> > E. Christian fellowship   4:7–18

OVERVIEW

Most of the New Testament letters have at least these three kinds of content: personal remarks or concerns, teaching and practical advice. The personal sections, involving people in the churches or individuals being written to, usually appear at the beginning and end of the letter. The teaching sections come before the practical, because the writer wanted first to point out God's truth and rules for living so that he could apply this truth to the real experiences of the first readers. Below, we can see how Colossians contains *all* of the content types:

MAINLY PERSONAL	MAINLY TEACHING		MAINLY PRACTICAL	MAINLY PERSONAL
Christian Thanksgiving	True Beliefs	False Beliefs	Christian Living	Christian Fellowship
CHRIST YOUR INHERITANCE	CHRIST LIVING IN YOU	CHRIST YOUR FOUNDATION	CHRIST YOUR GOAL	CHRIST YOUR MASTER
1:1	1:13	2:6	3:1	4:7

When a letter like Colossians exposes false teaching, it will first present the *truths that are being violated* and then expose the false beliefs by comparison.

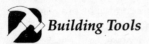 *Building Tools*

IMPORTANT PASSAGES

• *Thanksgiving and intercession* (1:3–12). Look at what Paul is thankful for and his desires for the Colossians, in light of the danger confronting the church. How are the things he prays about and for still important today?

• *Person and work of Christ* (1:13–2:5). The phrases around the repeated word "all" in 1:15–20 show much about Jesus, because later in the letter, Paul will expose the false teaching in the church. As you study the nouns, verbs and connecting words in this section, be attentive to the majestic portrait of Christ Paul is painting.

• *Heresies exposed* (2:6–23). These are the false teachings cited above. Although Paul never actually *names* them, see if you can locate the verses that describe each of the ones listed in the "Purpose" section.

• *Christianity in action* (3:1–4:18). Make a list of all the commands Paul issues in this section. Then see if you can group the commands under common headings using one-word titles.

KEY WORDS

all,[129] knowledge,[130] prayer

---

[129] This word is important because the false teachers were seeking to convince the Colossians that they were missing something in their Christian experience. They were being told that there was "more" and that they *didn't* have it "all."

[130] This word is important because the false teachers told the Colossians that the thing they were missing the most was "knowledge" of a special and secret nature.

1 THESSALONIANS
The Lord Jesus Is Coming Again

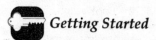 *Getting Started*

Jesus' first coming to earth was an event of great importance. His second coming will be the climax of world history. He came the first time to die and conquer death. When he comes again, it will be to gather to himself those who belong to him, and to rule as their King. In the two Thessalonian letters, Paul focused on the theme of Christ's return. The apostle not only gave many specific details of final events, but he also showed how Christians' awareness of the Lord's return should affect the way they live daily. We can't read or study these letters without growing stronger in our Christian faith and the lifestyle it produces.

AUTHOR AND DATE

Paul claims authorship at the very outset of the letter (1:1). Timothy and Silas are with him when he writes. Paul wrote this letter from Corinth around A.D. 51–52, after the letter to the Galatians, making 1 Thessalonians his earliest letter to an individual church.

FIRST READERS

Thessalonica was the capital city of the Roman province of Macedonia (see map on page 302). It was a free city located at the head of a gulf and so was also an important centre for trade. On Paul's second missionary journey he visited this gulf city and preached regularly in its synagogue. During this time he founded the Thessalonian church. He and his companions were driven out of Thessalonica by jealous Jews.[131] Paul sent Silas and Timothy back to Thessalonica to see how the young Christians were doing.[132] The report he received while at Corinth in Greece

[131] Acts 17:1-10
[132] 1 Thessalonians 3:1-6

prompted him to write the letter we know as 1 Thessalonians.

PURPOSE

Apparently, the report brought to Paul by Silas and Timothy regarding the Thessalonian church revealed some problems that needed attention, including:

(1) Encouragement in the face of persecution
(2) Instructions about personal holiness
(3) Warnings about sexual immorality
(4) Instructions about how the Lord's return relates to the life and death of Christians

THEME

The Lord Jesus is coming again.

KEY VERSES

"May your whole spirit, soul and body be kept sound and blameless at the coming of our Lord Jesus Christ. The one who calls you is faithful and he will do it" (5:23–24).

 First Reading

Paul's greeting and conclusion are both very brief,[133] supporting the idea that he wrote with the primary goal of meeting the immediate needs revealed to him by his two helpers upon their return.

OUTLINE
Jesus Is Coming Again

Greeting   1:1
Looking back   1:2–3:13
    A. Conversion and testimony   1:2–2:16
    B. Paul's service to them   2:17–3:13
Looking forward   4:1–5:24
    A. Their daily walk   4:1–12
    B. The Lord's return   4:13–5:24
Conclusion   5:25–28

---

[133] see 1:1 and 5:25-28

OVERVIEW

First Thessalonians is brief enough to read through in a single sitting. The following chart can give us some direction as we read the letter:

SALUTATION 1:1	LOOKING BACK			LOOKING FORWARD		CONCLUSION 5:25-28
	Thessalonians' Turning to Christ	Paul's Service		Daily Walk	Final Day of the Lord Will Come	
	1:2	2:1	3:1	4:1	4:13	

Paul has arranged his material with a backward and forward glance. Below are some key phrases from each section that show his emphasis on the past and the future:

- *Looking back* (1:2–3:13)

    "You *became* a model to all the believers"(1:7)
    "We *were* gentle among you"(2:7)
    "We *sent* Timothy . . . to strengthen and encourage you"(3:2)

- *Looking forward* (4:1–5:24). Paul indicates his change of focus quite clearly in this section:

    "Now we ask you and urge you in the Lord Jesus *to do this* more and more"(4:1)
    "The Lord himself *will come* down from heaven"(4:16)
    "The dead in Christ *will rise* first"(4:16)
    "After that, we who are still alive and are left *will be caught up* together with them in the clouds to meet the Lord in the air. And so *we will be* with the Lord for ever'' (4:17)
    "This day *should [not] surprise you* like a thief"(5:4)

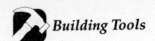

Building Tools

IMPORTANT PASSAGES

Don't let the brevity of this letter fool you. It is rich for study. For this letter, study only the verbs, particularly the commands Paul gives. Set up a chart like the one below and work your way through the book slowly, giving thought especially to the third column of your chart:

COMMAND	CHAPTER/ VERSE	WHY THIS COMMAND IS IMPORTANT TO ME
"Thank"	1:2	thanksgiving causes me to focus on the Lord
_____	_____	_____
_____	_____	_____
_____	_____	_____
_____	_____	_____

KEY WORDS

brothers, coming, word, love

2 THESSALONIANS
The Day of the Lord Has Not Yet Come

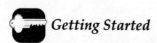 *Getting Started*

After Paul wrote 1 Thessalonians, some of the people in the church got the wrong idea about his teaching on the coming "day of the Lord" in the clouds to "take up" (i.e., rapture) the saints, dead and living, to heaven.[134] Then, the Thessalonians spread the word that "the day" had *already* come[135] and that was why they were experiencing persecution.[136] There was even the strong probability that someone had written the church with these teachings, *claiming to be Paul!*[137]

Paul wanted to correct these wrong beliefs by saying that the time of eternal punishment was yet to come.[138] So, he wrote a second letter to the church in Thessalonica.

AUTHOR AND DATE

Paul's name appears twice in this letter, claiming authorship in both places,[139] and that *this* letter was authentic! He probably wrote this second letter about six months after the first one, which would place it around A.D. 52 from Corinth. (NOTE: These are the only two letters Paul wrote while on his second missionary journey.)

FIRST READERS

Paul wrote this letter to the same people addressed in his first letter, new Christians in the city of Thessalonica.

---

[134] Read 1 Thessalonians 4:13-18 again.
[135] 2 Thessalonians 2:2
[136] 1:4
[137] see 2:1–2
[138] 1:7-10
[139] 1:1 and 3:17

PURPOSE

The letter praises the Thessalonian Christians for their growing faith in the face of persecution, assures them of his prayer support, and seeks to correct the false understanding that had arisen regarding what he had taught concerning the "day of the Lord" in his first letter to them. In this letter, Paul argues that the "day of the Lord" had not already come. Therefore, they should not be disturbed or confused over their suffering. They should stand strong and continue to believe the teachings he gave them and work productively in the meantime.[140]

THEME

The day of the Lord will *not* arrive until after "the man of lawlessness" has appeared.

KEY VERSES

"The coming of the lawless one will be in accordance with the work of Satan displayed in all kinds of counterfeit miracles, signs and wonders, and in every sort of evil that deceives those who are perishing. They perish because they refused to love the truth and so be saved" (2:9–10).

 First Reading

Once again, Paul keeps his greeting and "sign–off" very brief, indicating that his primary motive in writing was instructional more than personal.[141]

OUTLINE

The Day of the Lord Has Not Come Yet

    Greeting   1:1–2
        A. Don't be disturbed   1:3–12
        B. Stand firm   2:1–17
        C. Work hard until he comes   3:1–15
    Conclusion   3:16–18

---

[140] 1:3-10; 2:13-17; 3:6-15
[141] see 1:1–2 and 3:16-18

OVERVIEW

The entire letter consists of merely forty-seven verses, but it is interesting to note that eighteen of these are about end times. This reinforces our understanding of the letter's primary purpose. Paul told them in 1 Thessalonians that the Lord Jesus is coming again. This letter says he hasn't come yet.

Read through 2 Thessalonians with the aid of the survey chart below:

2 THESSALONIANS: THE DAY OF THE LORD HAS NOT COME YET

SALUTATION 1:1-2	PERSECUTION - commendation	PROPHECY - correction	PRACTICE - exhortation	CONCLUSION 3:16-18
	DON'T BE DISTURBED	DAY OF THE LORD NOT YET STAND FIRM	WORK	
	1:3 LORD IN GLORY	2:1 MAN OF SIN	3:1 MODEL OF WORKER	

As you read the text of 2 Thessalonians slowly, pay careful attention to Paul's comments on the subjects below:

• *The Lord in glory* (1:3–12). Paul showed how Christians are involved in Christ's glory. We look to see how persecutions are related to that glory (1:4–10).

• *The man of evil* (2:1–17). This is the Antichrist of the end times. Paul wrote that the day of the Lord will not come until two things have happened: first, a great rebellion against God will occur (2:3). Second, the "man of lawlessness" will appear, the one who will encourage rebellion against God. Chapter 2 is the key chapter of this letter, and we should spend much time in it. Take time to become familiar with the characteristics of this "man of lawlessness" because Paul had told them earlier that "this day should [not] surprise you like a thief"(1 Th. 5:4).

• *Work until he comes* (3:6–15). Much is written in this letter about the importance of work as it relates to persecution, the Antichrist and the "day of the Lord." Why does Paul spend so much time talking about work when he is giving such clear teaching on the "day of the Lord?" Perhaps there is a strong clue here regarding what our *focus* should be in the meantime.

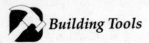 *Building Tools*

IMPORTANT PASSAGES

Two valuable themes that can be gleaned from this letter are suffering and the characteristics of evil. Look at the passages below, paying special attention to the adjectives used to describe the causes and effects of suffering, and the description of evil personified in the Antichrist. Then, compare *your* response to suffering and *your* own character. What encouragement can you find? What correction should you make?

- Suffering—1:3–12; 2:16; 3:3
- Characteristics of evil—2:3–12

KEY WORDS

Lord, pray, evil

1 TIMOTHY
Pastors and People in Churches

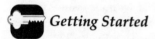 *Getting Started*

The Man Called Timothy
Timothy was a young man who had joined Paul on his second missionary journey when he was in the city of Lystra in Galatia (see map on page 302). Timothy's mother, Eunice, was a Jew and his father a Greek. He accompanied Paul on his third missionary journey[142] and as we have seen, was present with him in Rome when he wrote his four "prison letters." By and large, this young man was Paul's "right hand". There is even good evidence that Paul was the one who led Timothy to the Lord.[143]

The Letter to Timothy
In order to understand much of the language and themes of this letter, we need to go back to Paul's third missionary journey, when he and his helper Timothy spent about three years preaching and teaching the gospel in Ephesus and the surrounding area.[144] After he returned to Jerusalem, Paul was sent to prison in Rome.[145] While there, he sent the Ephesian church a letter praising the people for their holy walk with the Lord.[146] But soon Paul began to hear reports of problems that were hurting the churches in that area.

After Paul was released from prison, he and Timothy visited the churches around Ephesus and saw the problems firsthand. Paul asked Timothy to stay on at Ephesus and shepherd the Christians there, working out the problems in the process.[147] Be-

---

[142] Acts 16:1-4
[143] 1 Timothy 1:2; 2 Timothy 1:2; 1 Corinthians 4:17
[144] Acts 18:23-21:17
[145] Acts 21:18-28:31
[146] Ephesians 1:15–16
[147] 1:3

cause he would not be able to reach Ephesus when planned, Paul
wrote to his young helper.[148] Paul wanted Timothy and the
pastors and church leaders to face their spiritual enemies head-
on, in the power of God. We call this letter a "pastoral letter,"
although Timothy did not pastor a church alone, but worked as
Paul's helper.

FIRST READERS

The letter is addressed to Timothy, so we must assume that he
was Paul's "target," but we also can assume that Paul had a wider
audience in mind because he instructed Timothy to "Point these
things out to the brothers"(4:6).

PURPOSE

Paul wrote this letter to Timothy with three primary goals in
mind:

(1) *To encourage Timothy*. He was apparently having a
    somewhat difficult time in his role of training leaders.
    Paul wants to help him "keep going."
(2) *To warn Timothy*. Paul, the veteran leader, wants
    Timothy to be aware of the types of false teachers
    around and the methods they use. False doctrine was
    one of Paul's greatest enemies and he wants to equip
    Timothy to "fight the good fight" like him.
(3) *To instruct Timothy*. Paul gives him very specific in-
    structions on how a church ought to function, includ-
    ing the role of women, the selection of leadership and
    the care of widows.

THEME

Christians must watch their lives, deeds and teaching with
great care. It is the role of leaders to assure that they are equipped
and able.

KEY VERSE

"Timothy, guard what has been entrusted to your care. Turn
away from godless chatter and the opposing ideas of what is
falsely called knowledge"(6:20).

---

[148] 3:14-15

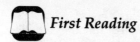

First Reading

Paul opens and closes this letter to his dear fellow labourer with short benedictions of good wishes. The letter begins and ends with Paul's clear endorsement of Timothy.[149]

OUTLINE
Pastors and People in Churches

Greeting   1:1–2
Commands to Timothy   1:3–20
    A. Sound doctrine   1:3–11
    B. Grace and warfare   1:12–20
Instructions to Timothy   2:1–6:21a
    A. Public worship in the church   2:1–15
    B. Church leaders   3:1–13
    C. A hymn of worship   3:14–16
    D. Help to fight false teaching   4:1–16
    E. Widows, elders and slaves   5:1–6:2a
    F. Final instructions   6:2b–21a
Blessing   6:21b

OVERVIEW

Paul's first letter to Timothy clearly pivots around the idea of the local church. Paul presents Timothy with instructions regarding "rules" for how a church should function, and "pastoral help" for shepherding God's people in the midst of a functioning church. The book can be diagrammed as follows:

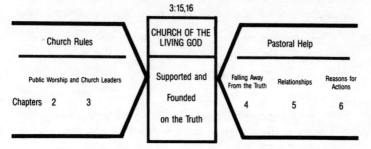

---

[149] 1:1–2; 6:21

• *Public worship and church leaders* (chapters 2 and 3). Here, Paul provides Timothy with broad principles for worship and specific qualifications for church leaders. This section contains the clearest and most rigorous description of a church leader in the New Testament. We would do well in our day to heed Paul's counsel to Timothy.

• *Pastoral help* (chapters 4–6). In this section, Timothy receives instruction regarding false teachers and Timothy's responsibility to the truth, widows and slaves and the local fellowship's responsibility to them, and finally, proper incentives for living, especially mentioning the issue of financial success. As in the previous sections, Paul's advice is virtually ''timeless.''

Building Tools

IMPORTANT PASSAGES

This letter contains three "hymns" that are worth study and meditation. Read the paragraph *prior* to each of the verses below in your study.

    HYMN #1   ''Honour and glory for ever!'' (1:17)
    HYMN #2   The "mystery of godliness"(3:16)
    HYMN #3   "King of Kings"(6:15–16)

Another source of rich biblical treasure is in Paul's description of a godly leader in 3:1–13. Although he speaks primarily of men here, the traits he lists are equally desirable for any Christian who wants to grow. Make a list of the traits and meditate on each. Perhaps use the cross-references in your Bible to find mention or descriptions of each trait elsewhere in the New Testament. How did Jesus fulfil them all?

KEY WORDS

teach, serve, command, love

2 TIMOTHY
Endurance and Separation

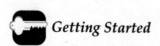 *Getting Started*

This is the last letter Paul wrote. It is tender and loving. Paul was an old man, living out his final hours in a cold, dark, Roman dungeon. Knowing he only has a short time left in this life, Paul pens this letter, a spiritual last will and testament of sorts. It is his "dying wish" to his faithful friend and co-worker, Timothy.

Approximately five years have transpired since Paul's first letter to Timothy. One very significant difference is that Paul is no longer a free man! Christians throughout the Roman Empire were now suffering for their faith. The cruel Emperor Nero was hostile towards the followers of Jesus. He would have liked nothing better than to wipe out Christianity altogether. He was partially successful, or so he thought. He had the church's dauntless leader Paul behind bars and was planning his imminent death. Tradition tells us that Paul was kept in the infamous Mamertine Prison, probably in solitary confinement. His cell's only entrance was in the ceiling. Once inside, the nineteen-by-ten-foot cell left little room for movement—it was only 6 1/2 feet high!

The first time Paul was imprisoned in Rome (A.D. 58–62), he expected to be set free.[150] It is clear from this letter that he expects to be killed.[151]

AUTHOR AND DATE

Paul clearly states that he is the author of this letter. Because we know that the Emperor Nero died in June, A.D. 68, it is likely that this letter can be dated *prior* to that. A.D. 67 is generally the accepted date.

---

[150] see Paul's "prison epistle" Philippians 1:24-26
[151] 4:6

FIRST READERS

The entire letter is essentially Paul's "farewell" to a beloved and trusted friend. In the letter, however, we also find short messages Paul wanted Timothy to deliver to others. The last short blessing, "Grace be with you [plural]"[152] was intended for everyone who knew the apostle.

PURPOSE

Paul wrote out of a lonely heart, saying a genuine and warm "good-bye" to one who was perhaps his dearest friend. His main *spiritual* purpose was to stimulate, inspire, and challenge Timothy to keep going with the gospel ministry. He also wanted Timothy to visit him in Rome before winter, probably because navigation ceased then, and Paul apparently did not expect to live much longer than that.[153]

THEME

Christian workers approved by the Lord endure problems, avoid evil people, make known the Good News, and teach the Word of God.

KEY VERSES

"But the Lord stood at my side and gave me strength, so that through me the message might be fully proclaimed and all the Gentiles might hear it. And I was delivered from the lion's mouth. The Lord will rescue me from every evil attack and will bring me safely to his heavenly kingdom. To him be glory for ever and ever. Amen" (4:17–18).

 First Reading

After reading the letter we can understand why it has been called "a letter mixed with gloom and glory." There is tenderness and sadness in such lines as these:

- "Recalling your tears" (1:4)
- "Do not be ashamed . . . of me" (1:8)

---

[152] 4:22
[153] see 4:6–9, 21

- "Everyone deserted me" (4:16)
- "The time has come for my departure" (4:6)

But the main tone of the letter, even when talking about suffering, is triumph, glory, and deep thankfulness:

- "By the power of God" (1:8)
- "You, however, know all about my teaching, my way of life, my purpose, faith, patience, love, endurance" (3:10)
- "There is in store for me the crown of righteousness" (4:8)
- "To him be glory for ever and ever" (4:18)

BEGINNING AND END

The greeting is brief,[154] almost as if Paul is anxious to get on with what he has to say. But the end of the letter is long. There are personal words, instructions and testimonies,[155] followed by greetings and a benediction.[156] We hold in our hands the final letter of a man of God. Even though Paul was assured that his destination was the presence of God, it is obvious that his heart is full of love towards his friends, especially Timothy.

OUTLINE
Endurance and Separation

    Salutation   1:1–2
        A. Challenge to share in suffering   1:3–2:13
        B. Challenge to separate from evil people   2:14–4:5
        C. Parting words   4:6–8
        D. Personal instructions   4:9–18
    Greetings and benediction   4:19–22

OVERVIEW

The main body of the letter, leading to a climax in 4:6–8, presents two challenges to the first readers: a challenge to share in sufferings and a challenge to separate from evil people.

---

[154] 1:1–2
[155] 4:9-18
[156] 4:19-22

2 TIMOTHY: ENDURANCE AND SEPARATION

	1:3	2:1	2:14	4:1	4:6	4:9	4:18	
SALUTATION 1:1-2	CHALLENGE OF <u>FELLOWSHIP</u> OF SUFFERING		CHALLENGE OF <u>SEPARATION</u> FROM EVIL PEOPLE		PAUL'S PARTING WORDS	Personal Instructions		**GREETINGS AND BENEDICTION 4:19-22**
	thanksgiving	exhortation	warning	charge	TESTIMONY OF TRIUMPH			
	"I thank God for you"	"Be strong"	"More and more away from God"	"Preach the Good News"				

• *Challenge to share in suffering* (1:3–2:13). The key messages are, "Join with me in suffering" (1:8) and "Endure hardship with us like a good soldier of Christ Jesus" (2:3). Paul could patiently accept all the troubles that resulted from the gospel ministry, knowing the end result was the salvation of men (2:10). Now, he challenges Timothy to adopt the same vision, to suffer if necessary, "for the gospel" (1:8).

• *Challenge to separate from evil people* (2:14–4:5). The key message here is, "Have nothing to do with them" (3:5). This entire paragraph outlines the different sins of these evil people.[157] Paul exhorted Timothy to follow the scriptural path he had been taught since childhood from his mother and other teachers. Paul gave him these instructions: "Preach the Word; be prepared in season and out of season . . . do the work of an evangelist, discharge all the duties of your ministry" (4:2,5). We see here that Paul draws Timothy's attention to his own past in an attempt to provide the encouragement he needed.

We see that this letter moves toward a climax, which is the stirring testimony of Paul himself (4:6–8). He had finished the race, and now a crown was waiting for him. This final letter to Timothy is intended to remind him that "finishing" is the goal, not merely "running."

---

[157] 3:1-9

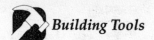 *Building Tools*

IMPORTANT PASSAGES

Even though this letter is intensely personal, it contains a number of brief passages that are worth further study. Look at them, taking special note of the suggestions included with each:

Characteristics of the "last days" 3:1–9,13
- The orientation of people (inward vs. outward)
- The perspective on authority
- What they "love" and don't love
- The obsession with knowledge and learning
- The false religiosity

The Scriptures 3:16–17
- Their source and why that is important
- Their "usefulness"

Paul's farewell 4:1–22
- What has been important to him in life
- His perspective on people (even those who failed him)
- Why he has done what he has with his life

KEY WORDS

suffer, ashamed, Word/Scriptures, endure, work(er)

TITUS
Doing Good Deeds

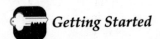 **Getting Started**

No one can be saved *by* good works, but good works have a valid and important place in the Christian's life. This New Testament book has much to say on the subject.

The Man, Titus

After Paul's release from his first Roman imprisonment, he wrote *two* letters to fellow labourers in the gospel. One was to his closest friend, Timothy.[158] The second was to a man named Titus. Paul and Titus must have done evangelistic work in towns on the island of Crete, south of Greece (see map on page 302), because in this letter, Paul says he "left him there."[159]

Timothy and Titus were alike in many ways—both were young, gifted co-workers of Paul, probably even converted under the apostle's ministry.[160] Both also served as Paul's representatives in difficult churches on the Mediterranean. It is interesting to note that although obviously a companion and friend of Paul, Titus' name does not appear anywhere in the book of Acts. We have only this book and some sketchy mentions elsewhere to formulate what we know of him. Yet, we can assume that he was a competent and loyal disciple of Christ, or Paul would never have left him in charge of a group of churches.

The Island of Crete

Crete is a mountainous island in the Mediterranean Sea. It measures about 156 miles across and varies from 7–35 miles in width. Luke tells us that Paul's ship stopped at this island on its

---

[158] This would be our New Testament book, 1 Timothy.
[159] 1:5
[160] 1 Timothy 1:2; Titus 1:4

voyage to Rome with Paul as its prisoner.[161]

The Cretan people had a bad reputation in the Mediterranean world. Paul alludes to this in Titus when he says: "Cretans are always liars, evil brutes, lazy gluttons" (1:12). Some of these people had become Christians, and Paul wanted to encourage them to *live* like Christians. "For the grace of God that brings salvation has appeared to all men. It teaches us to say 'No' to ungodliness and worldly passions, and to live self-controlled, upright and godly lives in this present age" (2:11–12). Over and over again in the letter, Paul wrote about doing good deeds. When we consider the background of many of those in the churches, we can understand his motive and the need.

AUTHOR AND DATE

Because of the similarity to 1 Timothy, it is very likely that Paul wrote these two letters within a short time of one another. He probably wrote to Titus around A.D. 62, while en route to the city of Nicopolis in northern Macedonia, where he was hoping to spend the winter.[162]

FIRST READERS

Although the letter is addressed to Titus, like 1 Timothy, we may assume that Paul had a wider audience in mind as well,[163] namely the Cretan church.

PURPOSE

Paul penned this second "pastoral" letter with two primary goals in mind:

(1) To remind Titus that his task is to supervise the churches.
(2) To encourage the Cretan Christians about *doing good deeds* in everyday living.

Another minor purpose was Paul's desire to have Titus try to meet him in Nicopolis where Paul was planning to spend the winter.

---

[161] see Acts 27:7ff
[162] 3:12
[163] "you must teach . . ."(2:1), and "Remind the people . . ."(3:1)

KEY VERSES

"We lived in malice and envy, being hated and hating one another. But when the kindness and love of God our Saviour appeared, he saved us, not because of righteous things we had done, but because of his mercy" (3:3–5).

 First Reading

The opening greeting is simple—"From Paul . . . To Titus" (1:1,4)—but between these comments is a beautiful statement about preaching God's truth to the world. The conclusion of the letter has the usual personal notes, but is accompanied by a final statement by Paul on the theme of the letter—*doing good deeds*. [164]

OUTLINE
Doing Good Deeds

> Introduction   1:1–4
>> A. Leaders of an orderly church   1:5–16
>> B. Members of a sound church   2:1–15
>> C. Members of a practising church   3:1–11
>
> Conclusion   3:12–15

OVERVIEW

Paul's thoughts in this letter are all centred around the theme of a "healthy" church. His ideas may be divided like this:

- An orderly church—a healthy church consists of competent leaders and willing followers.
- A sound church—a healthy church must be built upon order and truth.
- A practising church—a healthy church consists of members whose life-style is characterized by good deeds.

---

[164] 3:12-15

INTRODUCTION 1:1-4	LEADERS 1:5		LAITY 2:1	- old - young - slaves - masters	GENERAL 3:1	CONCLUSION 3:12-15
	Orderly Church		Sound Church Built on Truth		Practising Church	
	leaders	opponents (10)	followers			

Building Tools

IMPORTANT PASSAGES

Below are three of the passages in Titus deserving of more detailed attention. Examine what Paul has to say to Titus and how and why it is vital for us today.

- False teaching in a church   1:1–16
- Making the gospel attractive   2:1–10
- The grace of God   2:11–14; 3:4–7

KEY WORDS

doing good (deeds), teach(ing), grace

PHILEMON
An Appeal for Forgiveness

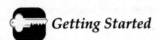 *Getting Started*

A forgiving spirit is so important that Jesus included forgiveness in the prayer he taught his disciples.[165] Paul also believed that forgiveness was a way of showing Christian love. This emphasis on forgiveness was the reason he wrote to his friend Philemon. Picture, if you will, the setting that prompted this letter from Paul's pen:

Philemon was a well-to-do Christian friend of Paul, living in or near the city of Colosse. He was more than likely a member of the small Colossian church, to whom Paul had also written. It appears from this letter that one of Philemon's slaves, Onesimus, had stolen something from his master and fearing punishment, fled to Rome. The size of the Empire's capital made it relatively easy for a runaway slave to get "lost in the crowd." Onesimus would run little risk of recapture.

But, while in Rome, Onesimus came to know Paul while he was under house arrest, *and* he came to know Jesus Christ as his 'Saviour.[166] Now, Paul was concerned that Onesimus get back to Philemon, his master, *but also now his brother in the Lord!* Paul doesn't want Onesimus to be punished, so he wrote this tender and moving letter to ask Philemon to forgive and free his slave-become-brother. This is the only one of Paul's strictly personal letters that is preserved for us in the New Testament. The letter was carried to Philemon by Onesimus himself and Tychicus, who also delivered the letters known as Ephesians and Colossians to the churches in those cities.

---

[165] see Matthew 6:12
[166] Acts 28:16,30–31 tells of Paul's imprisonment and the ministry he had while under house arrest. Philemon 10 hints that Onesimus had come to saving faith in Christ as a result of Paul.

AUTHOR AND DATE

Paul wrote the letter, sending Timothy's greetings in its opening verse. The apostle is still under house arrest in Rome during his first imprisonment there, making the date very near that of the other prison epistles, A.D. 61.

FIRST READERS

The letter has Philemon as its primary recipient, but Paul also sent greetings to Philemon's wife Apphia, their son, Archippus, and to the church that met in their home.[167] This letter gives us a glimpse into what life was like in a first century household.

PURPOSE

Paul's primary purpose was to seek to secure Onesimus' reinstatement as a brother in the Lord, in the household of Philemon from which he had fled.

THEME

The letter rotates around one Christian's plea to another Christian to forgive and restore a third party.

KEY VERSE

"If he has done you any wrong or owes you anything, charge it to me" (18).

 First Reading

Paul began and closed his letter in the usual style: an introductory greeting and blessing (1–3), concluded by personal notes, greetings, and another blessing (22–25). The letter is saturated with warmth and the bonds of friendship.

OUTLINE
An Appeal for Forgiveness

Greeting   1–3
    A. The object of the appeal   4–7
    B. The appeal itself   8–16

---

[167] verse 2

   C. The source of the appeal   17–21
   Conclusion and blessing   22–25

OVERVIEW

When we read this brief "postcard," we may be surprised at how *organized* a friendly, personal message can be. Follow the outline as you read the Bible text.

PHILEMON: APPEAL FOR FORGIVENESS

	OBJECT OF THE APPEAL: Philemon's love	THE APPEAL: for a new relationship	SOURCE OF THE APPEAL: Paul's love	
SALUTATION 1-3	praise of Philemon	plea for Onesimus	promise of Paul	CONCLUSION 22-25
	4	8	17 21	

• *Object of the appeal* (4–7). Paul asked for Philemon's help because of his Christian love and faith.

• *The appeal itself* (8–16). Paul told Philemon that Onesimus was a changed man now that he was a believer. (In this section, Paul makes a play on the word "useful" which is the meaning of Onesimus.) He tells Philemon why he would want to have Onesimus back; he is now a brother in Christ.

• *The source of the appeal* (17–21). Paul reminds Philemon of their friendship. He even goes so far as to hint that Philemon "owes" him a favour for some deed Paul had done.

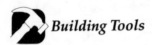 *Building Tools*

IMPORTANT PASSAGES

Two exciting themes that are illustrated by this brief letter are: forgiveness in general, and the work of Christ on behalf of sinners in particular. Go through the letter slowly and write down all the thoughts you can find regarding:

• Forgiveness—ours, God's, others (NOTE: the word "forgiveness" does not appear in the letter. Look for evidences and actions indicating forgiveness.)

- The work of Christ for you (Pay special attention to Paul's statements about what Philemon should do, why, and what Paul is willing to do.)

HEBREWS
Consider Jesus, Our Great High Priest

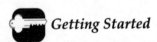 **Getting Started**

The book of Hebrews is a literary masterpiece. It shows how Christ fulfils the teaching, predictions, and requirements of the Old Testament. All the ceremonies, such as the priests' offerings of sacrifices, and even the Jewish priesthood itself, are shown to be "pictures" pointing forward to Christ. He is the fulfilment.

This letter was written because of a great spiritual need. The Jewish Christians addressed by the letter were losing sight of God's Son, the all-sufficient Saviour, and were turning more and more back to their old lifestyle. "Fix your thoughts on Jesus!" (3:1) is the urgent call issuing from its pages.

This exciting book is often called the "fifth Gospel" because it tells of Jesus' past work on earth and his present work in heaven.[168] Just as Jehovah God led the Israelites from Egypt to Canaan through all kinds of dangers and troubles, so today Christ is helping his children enter into the spiritual rest-land of a full life, giving a taste of heavenly glories yet to come.

It is possible that this letter was written at a time when persecution of Christians was beginning to accelerate worldwide. The Jewish Christians would have been severely tempted to return to the old Jewish religious system because of the freedom and safety it afforded. The book of Hebrews is a call to remember and rekindle the distinctive characteristics of Christianity.

AUTHOR AND DATE

The author of Hebrews is unstated and unknown. This is the only New Testament book whose author is not fixed. Paul, Barnabas, Apollos and another co-worker of Paul have all been suggested over the years as viable possibilities for authorship.

---

[168] 2:9 and 4:14

FIRST READERS

The letter was sent to a congregation of Jewish Christians[169] living somewhere in the Roman world. They probably resided in a major city such as Rome, Ephesus or Jerusalem. We are not told and do not know the specific location to which this letter was sent.

PURPOSE

The many strong warnings in the book indicate that the first readers were in a state of extreme spiritual need, turning from Christ as the focal point of their faith, back to their former Jewish beliefs. The author is attempting to re-light the embers of a dying fire through teaching, warning and encouraging—all centred on Jesus Christ. Even the opening lines show us the author's intent to present a single theme: "He has spoken to us by his Son"(1:2).

THEME

We have a great High Priest who is Jesus!

KEY VERSE

"Therefore, since we have a great high priest who has gone through the heavens, Jesus the Son of God, let us hold firmly to the faith we profess" (4:14).

 First Reading

We can get an early "feel" for this somewhat lengthy book by scanning its segment headings (added to your Bible) in one or two quick glances.

The book closes in what appears to be Paul's typical style— personal notes and blessings, and even a reference to Timothy![170] But its opening comments are totally *unlike* the apostle, containing no greeting at all.

---

[169]The book contains at least thirty Old Testament quotations, all taken from the Septuagint, the Greek version of the Old Testament. The multitude of references to the Jewish history (e.g. Moses, Joshua, etc.), the ceremonial system, and the typology employed (e.g. priest, sacrifice, tabernacle, etc.) leaves little doubt that the audience was comprised almost exclusively of converts from Judaism to Christianity.

[170] see 13:17-25, especially verse 23

The opening words provide an excellent synopsis of the book's theme:[171]

"God has spoken"	Revelation
"Through his Son"	The person Jesus
"[Who] sat down"	The finished work of Jesus

OUTLINE
Consider Jesus, Our Great High Priest

A. Superior Person is Jesus Christ   1:1–7:28
B. Superior work of Jesus Christ   8:1–10:18
C. Superior life in Jesus Christ   10:19–13:25

OVERVIEW

The organization of Hebrews is first instruction (1:1–10:18) and then application (10:19–13:25). The order of arrangement is intentional: the abundant or full life of the Christian is possible only because of the superior *person*, Jesus Christ, who lives in the believer. The result of the indwelling Christ is superior *help* to live a godly life.

• *What does the Christian have?* (ch 1–7). The material contained within these chapter details all the things that belong to those who belong to Christ.

• *Our great high priest* (8:1–10:18). This middle section begins with the affirmation, "We have such a High Priest," and from here the author explains the work of this superior High Priest, Jesus. There is none like him. No intercessor, no animal sacrifice, no priest compares with the incomparable Christ. After laying an indisputable foundation of the sufficiency and superiority of Christ, he moves to the final section of the book.

• *Abundant life in Christ* (10:19–13:25). Beginning with the admonition, "therefore . . .", the author leads the reader into a rich section of practical teaching on *how to live* as a result of what they now know.

---

[171] 1:2-3

HEBREWS: CONSIDER JESUS, OUR GREAT HIGH PRIEST

INSTRUCTION		APPLICATION
SUPERIOR PERSON	SUPERIOR MINISTRIES	ABUNDANT LIFE
"What have we?"	"We have <u>SUCH</u> A HIGH PRIEST"	"Having . . . therefore . . . <u>let us</u>"
1:1	8:1	10:19 13:25

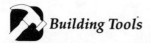 *Building Tools*

IMPORTANT PASSAGES

The letter to the Hebrews contains five clear "warnings." They are listed below. Examine each of them closely, paying special attention to what precedes and follows each. Take notes on why these warnings were necessary in the first century and why they are still important for us today.

The Warnings of Hebrews

2:1–4	"We must be more careful"
3:7–4:13	"Let us try hard to enter God's rest"
5:11–6:20	"Then they fell away from Christ!"
10:26–31	"There is no longer any sacrifice for sins"
12:25–29	"Do not refuse to listen when God speaks"

Another fruitful study awaits you in chapter eleven. It is called the "Hall of Faith" chapter. Read it carefully, taking note of what constitutes and characterizes genuine faith and what doesn't. Also, record what *our* expectations about life in general should be, if *we* desire to be men or women of faith.

KEY WORDS

better, high priest , perfect, eternal

JAMES
Faith and Works

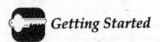 *Getting Started*

This book may very well have been the first New Testament book to be written. It contains the type of message God would have wanted his people to hear soon after Jesus ascended to his Father.

The Bible speaks mainly on two related themes: the way *to* God, and the way to walk *with* God. No one can walk or live day by day with God who has not first returned to Him. Much of the New Testament teaches the way to God—it is by God's grace, through faith in Jesus Christ. James tells his first readers about their walk with God. They are saved, but their faith must bring forth works. A faith that fails to show itself is "useless" and "dead," according to James.[172]

James wrote with authority. His letter is sharp and contains many penetrating and provocative truths. But his strong words were blended with personal warmth and love, because he knew his first readers were facing difficult times of persecution and suffering for their faith.

AUTHOR AND DATE

The writer calls himself James. We can infer from Scripture that this James was the half-brother of our Lord who became a believer shortly after Jesus' death.[173] Because this letter makes no clear mention of Gentiles and the writer uses the word "syna-

---

[172] 2:20, 26

[173] see Acts 1:14 and 1 Corinthians 15:7. There were four men in the New Testament with the name James. However, because of the attitude of authority that permeates this letter, we know *this* James must have been a recognized leader in the early church. Because the other James who was a leader (the brother of John) was martyred in A.D. 44 (see Acts 12:2), we can surmise that the only other possibility is James, the half-brother of Jesus.

gogue" for "meeting,"[174] we may assume a very early date, around A.D. 45–50.

FIRST READERS

James wrote to Jewish Christians "scattered among the nations" who were suffering for their faith in Jesus Christ. If the book was written early in the history of the church, it is possible that the first readers were among those in Jerusalem who were scattered after the stoning of Stephen. Although we are uncertain *when* they were scattered, we know with certainty that James is writing to *Jewish* Christians who had been dispersed.

We also can discern from this letter that James addresses roughly the same issue that Paul did in Galatians, namely the relationship between the works of the law and the life of faith. A significant difference is that Paul's first readers were seeking to be *justified by good deeds*, whereas James' first readers were feeling *exempted from good deeds because they were justified*. Knowing this distinction is essential to understanding the apparent conflict between these two New Testament books. They addressed different problems centred around the same issue.

PURPOSE

The book contains many subjects, indicating that James was writing for several reasons, including the following:

- To encourage Christians who were facing persecution
- To correct wrong doctrine about faith and works
- To instruct on proper Christian behaviour.

THEME

Genuine faith produces good works.

KEY VERSE

"As the body without the spirit is dead, so faith without deeds is dead"(2:26).

---

[174] 2:2

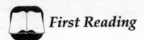 *First Reading*

The brief greeting and absence of any formal conclusion tell us that James wanted to get to "the business at hand" with this letter. This is consistent with the Jewish mind which was immensely practical and straightforward.

OUTLINE
Faith and Works

> Greeting   1:1
> > A. Faith in testings   1:2–18
> > B. Faith at work   1:19–4:12
> > C. Faith that is idle   4:13–5:12
> > D. Faith in the fellowship   5:13–20

OVERVIEW

Because it is difficult to see a clear pattern in the things James discusses from paragraph to paragraph, the outline above focuses on a broad subject: *faith*. Below is a second way to view the book, with *works* as the focus. It is clear that this letter informs about the indispensable union of faith and works in the life of an authentic believer. As we read each paragraph of the letter, we should try to identify its connection with both of these broad themes.

- *Motives for works* (1:2–18). Our willingness to give in the midst of trials is proof of the genuineness of our faith.
- *Importance of works* (1:19–4:12). James shows his first readers that even their "father" Abraham had a faith evidenced by works, and pinpoints their speech and conduct with one another as two prime targets for "good works."
- *Judgment of works* (4:13–5:12). James provides a sobering exhortation to his first readers to be careful how they plan their lives and treat the poor among them.
- *Ministry of works* (5:13–20). Prayer is highlighted as a valid and effective type of "works."

JAMES: FAITH AND WORKS

	FAITH IN TESTINGS	FAITH AT WORK	FAITH AND THE FUTURE	FAITH AND OUR FELLOWSHIP	
SALUTATION 1:1	motives for works	the place of works	judgment of works	outreach of works	
	1:2	1:19	4:13	5:13	5:20

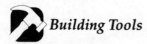 *Building Tools*

IMPORTANT PASSAGES

Because of its immensely practical nature, James is a book worth many hours of studying. Over one half of its 108 verses are commands, so there is plenty to apply! Below are four broad topics that are in James. As you read them, think carefully about *why* James says what he does. Think of the consequences for failure to apply these truths.

- The testing of our faith 1:1–18
- Authentic saving faith 2:14–26
- Controlling the tongue 3:1–12
- Living peacefully with each other 3:13–4:12

KEY WORDS

faith, deeds, judge

1 PETER
Hard Times, Holy Living, Christ's Coming

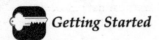 **Getting Started**

In the year A.D. 64, Emperor Nero decided to exterminate Christianity. News of those killed in the capital city of Rome spread quickly. Would the fires of suffering and persecution ignite the surrounding areas and spread into Asia Minor? Many of these believers had already left their homes in Jerusalem when persecution broke out there.[175] Now, in a foreign land, they were suffering difficult times, especially from unbelievers living around them.[176]

Things could only worsen. Peter did not write this letter to tell these Christians they were immune from further persecution. Instead, he encouraged them to stand true and endure the suffering for the sake of Christ and in his strength, no matter how intense it became. He seeks to change their focus from the difficulties at hand to the glory to come. The ideas of suffering and hope saturate this letter. Just thirty years later, when the apostle John wrote Revelation, it is clear that harsh persecution had indeed come to the Christians in Asia Minor.

AUTHOR AND DATE

The apostle Peter, one of the original twelve disciples and respected leader of the church in Jerusalem is the author of this letter.[177] Peter was martyred under Nero's Persecution in A.D. 68. Also, he seems to make a reference to Paul's "Prison Epistles" in his second letter,[178] which puts the date of this letter somewhere around A.D. 64.

---

[175] 1:6–7
[176] 2:11–12
[177] see 1:1 and 5:1
[178] 2 Peter 3:15

FIRST READERS

Peter states in his opening comments that he is writing to the *Christians* of Asia Minor. He specifically mentions large geographical areas. There are many quotations from the Old Testament, which would seem to indicate a Jewish audience. But Peter also mentions idolatry, a sin the Jews never fell into after the Babylonian Captivity in the sixth century B.C. This would point to Gentile first readers as well. Peter's first readers were probably a mixture of Jews and Gentiles, many of them natives of Judah, driven from their homes because of their Christian faith. [179]

PURPOSE

Peter's first readers were being persecuted and were *suffering* simply because they were Christians. Peter reminds them that their real hope is in the life to come. He encourages them to endure hardship and live godly lives in the meantime, awaiting the return of Christ.

THEME

God's people are to be noted for their holy living in an unholy world, prompted and strengthened by their hope in the second coming of Jesus Christ.

KEY VERSES

"The end of all things is near. Therefore, be clear minded and self-controlled so that you can pray. Above all, love each other deeply because love covers a multitude of sins"(4:7–8).

 First Reading

Peter's letter begins with majesty. Between the greeting (1:1) and the blessing (1:2) are three phrases highlighting the work of the three Persons of the Godhead in a Christian's salvation. Pondering these sweeping statements will encourage us as often as we read them.

The end of the letter is warm and inspiring as well: "...I have written to you briefly, encouraging you and testifying that this is the true grace of God"(5:12).

---

[179] see Acts 8:2-4

OUTLINE
Hard Times, Holy Living, Christ's Coming

Introduction   1:1–2
    A. Hard times and salvation   1:3–12
    B. A life of holiness   1:13–25
    C. God's chosen people   2:1–10
    D. A life of submission   2:11–3:12
    E. Hard times and glory   3:13–5:11
Conclusion   5:12–14

OVERVIEW

Peter addresses his first readers as "God's elect" in the opening verse. This phrase gives us a clue to an overall theme of the letter: *God's chosen people*. This theme is rephrased for us in 2:9–10, and as such becomes an excellent "hinge" for the book. What precedes and follows this "hinge" is surprisingly similar on both sides:

• *How they should live* (1:13–25 and 2:11–3:12). Peter addresses the same topic on both sides of the 2:9 "hinge."

• *How they should "look"* (1:3–12 and 3:13–5:11). On both sides of how they should live, Peter gives sound instruction on their perspective on trials, how they should "look" at life's difficulties.

Peter's arrangement of material is charted for you below:

1 PETER: TRIALS, HOLY LIVING, AND THE LORD'S COMING

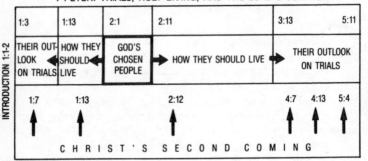

Building Tools

IMPORTANT PASSAGES

Peter's themes of suffering and hope produce some related themes worth following further. Two of them are:

- Holy living—Rather than simply looking up the verses that deal with holiness, meditate on the texts around them and ask yourself why this is so important for the Christian, especially a Christian who is suffering.
- Christ's return—There are six references in this letter to the return of Jesus. Find each of them and ponder their significance in themselves, *and* to one who is suffering.

KEY WORDS

suffer, holy, hope, glory

2 PETER
True and False Teaching

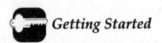 **Getting Started**

About three years after Peter wrote his first letter to the Christians in Asia Minor, he wrote again. Unlike his first letter where he addressed how they should respond to suffering from *without*, this second letter concerns itself almost exclusively with dangers from *within* the church.

Instead of facing trials brought on by those hostile to Christianity, the churches of Asia Minor were now facing serious attack from those who seemed to be "friendly" to the faith. False teachers were infiltrating the churches and turning many from the pure and sincere faith with which they had begun. Peter also wants to inform his first readers how to handle those who have rejected the Lord and his truth. Second Peter is a sobering reminder that the Christian faith always seems merely one generation from extinction! Knowing and guarding the truth are as important as seeking to live it.

AUTHOR AND DATE

The author identifies himself in the opening verse as "Simon Peter, a servant and apostle of Jesus Christ." We can surmise from the letter itself that Peter anticipates his own death shortly,[180] which would give us a date of about A.D. 67. Peter undoubtedly was writing from the city of Rome.

FIRST READERS

Peter makes it clear in the letter that he is writing to the same group that received his first letter a few years earlier.[181] There is some suggestion in his comment, "To those . . . who have received

---

[180] 1:14
[181] 3:1

a faith as precious as ours" that perhaps his audience includes some "new" first readers as well.

PURPOSE

Peter wrote this second letter for three reasons, and conveniently devotes a chapter to each:

(1) To urge Christian growth—chapter 1
(2) To identify false teaching—chapter 2
(3) To be looking for Christ's return —chapter 3

THEME

The one who claims to know God should guard himself against the teachings of false teachers *and* live their life looking forward to Christ's second coming.

KEY VERSE

"First of all, you must understand that in the last days scoffers will come, scoffing and following their own evil desires"(3:3).

 First Reading

Peter begins with a brief greeting and ends with a short sentence prayer of praise that highlights his motive for writing.[182]

OUTLINE
True and False Teaching

Greeting   1:1–2
    A. Try hard to grow   1:3–15
    B. Our Lord's powerful return   1:16–21
    C. Description of false teachers   2:1–22
    D. Judgment day is approaching   3:1–10
    E. New heavens and earth   3:11–16
Conclusion   3:17–18

OVERVIEW

Chapter 2 contains the "heart" of Peter's letter. It deals with

---

[182] 1:1–2 and 3:17–18

false teaching. He constructs the letter around this concern, with the paragraphs before and after dealing with *true* teaching. His words "try hard" surround this larger section on true and false teaching. The diagram below illustrates this arrangement:

2 PETER: TRUE AND FALSE PROPHECY

SALUTATION 1:1-2		PROPHECY				CONCLUSION 3:17-18
		TRUE	FALSE	TRUE		
	"TRY HARD"	powerful coming of our Lord	descriptions and prophecies of doom	day of God comes again	"TRY HARD"	
	1:3	1:16	2:1	3:1	3:11 3:16	

• *True teaching* (1:16–21). Peter points out that the important message of the Old Testament prophets was about the "power and coming of our Lord Jesus Christ," a "light shining in a dark place." Peter identifies the Holy Spirit as the agent of inspiration for these prophecies of the coming Messiah.

• *False prophecy* (2:1–22). In this section, Peter includes four paragraphs about false teachers:

    (1) A general statement about them   2:1–3
    (2) A warning of punishment   2:4–10a
    (3) Descriptions of evil people   2:10b–16
    (4) Destiny of evil people   2:17–22

• *True teaching* (3:1–10). Here is the most powerful message of this letter, a very vivid description of the signs surrounding the Lord's return. Peter describes the end of the physical world in stirring fashion.

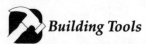 *Building Tools*

IMPORTANT PASSAGES

Below are some sections of Peter's letter that are excellent for further study. As you read and meditate on them, ask yourself how skilled *you* are in spotting and battling error. How prepared are *you* for the Lord's return? What is *your* focus as you wait for Christ? What is your *real* attachment to this physical world and its goods?

- Knowing God   1:1–11
- True and false teaching   1:12–3:10
- The end of the physical world   3:7–10
- Living in light of his coming   3:11–16

KEY WORDS

know, knowledge

1 JOHN
Fellowship with God and His Children

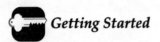 **Getting Started**

The writings of the apostle John, which include his Gospel, three short letters, and the book of Revelation, are the last five books of the Bible to be written. They were all composed some time between A.D. 85–100. It is generally accepted that the Gospel of John was the first and Revelation the last of the five.

What are the "marks" of a genuine Christian? What does true fellowship among believers consist of? Apparently near the close of the first century, the number of false teachers had increased and the basic "facts" of the gospel had been obscured. A clear apostolic statement was needed to show what constituted orthodoxy of belief and practice. John's first letter was God's answer to that need.

AUTHOR AND DATE

The author of this letter was John, a fisherman, and the "disciple Jesus loved."[183] Although none of the three short letters attributed to John actually bear his name, their similarity to his Gospel as well as the bulk of early church tradition that identifies him as their author, leaving no doubt as to who wrote them.

John was probably living in or around Ephesus where he spent the last years of his life preaching and teaching. When he was very old, John was exiled to the island of Patmos off the coast of Asia Minor.[184]

John is sometimes known as the apostle of love. His tender concern for other Christians is seen in his letters, where he often refers to his first readers as "my dear children" or "my dear friends." But he and his brother James were also called the "Sons

---

[183] see John 20:20
[184] see Revelation 1:9

of Thunder" by Jesus.[185] John was aggressive in ferreting out heresy and confronting it with the truth of God. This brief letter shows both the tender and tough sides of the apostle.

Because we know with some certainty when John died, we can fix a date of around A.D. 85–90 for this letter.

PURPOSE

John's first readers were facing a particular type of false teaching known as Gnosticism (pronounced "nosticism") which undercut essential Christian doctrine and behaviour. (It was preoccupied with a secret "knowledge" which is evident by how many times John uses the word "know" in this letter.) John wrote to strengthen their faith and fellowship by warning them about false teachers and the worldly activities that they promoted.

THEME

Christians can be assured of their salvation in Christ and enjoy fellowship with God and one another as a result.

KEY VERSES

"God is light; in him there is no darkness at all"(1:5). "Dear friends, let us love one another, . . ."(4:7). "I write these things . . . that you may know that you have eternal life"(5:13).

 First Reading

There is no formal greeting or conclusion. The use of "we" in the first paragraph may point to more than one writer, or the author may simply be saying "we" in a pastoral sense, as a way of including himself in what he's saying. His attachment to his first readers becomes obvious quite early in the letter, "my dear children"(2:1).

OUTLINE
Fellowship With God and His Children

      A. Participants of the fellowship   1:1–4
      B. Light of the fellowship   1:5–2:29
      C. Love of the fellowship   3:1–4:21

---

[185] Mark 3:17

D. Way to the fellowship   5:1–12
E. Certainty of the fellowship   5:13–21

OVERVIEW

Throughout the verses of 1 John the theme of fellowship recurs like a thread woven into a tapestry. The main core of the letter, 1:5–4:21, focuses on two descriptive statements, *God is light* and *God is love.* Use the chart below to aid you as you read this short but stirring letter.

1 JOHN: FELLOWSHIP WITH GOD AND HIS CHILDREN

''fellowship''	GOD IS LIGHT	GOD IS LOVE	''believe''	''know''	
PERSONS OF THE FELLOWSHIP	LIGHT OF FELLOWSHIP	LOVE OF FELLOWSHIP	WAY TO FELLOWSHIP	CERTAINTY OF FELLOWSHIP	
1:1	1:5	3:1	5:1	5:13	5:21

• *Participants of fellowship* (1:1–4). The repeated word "life" in this section is the key. The word "fellowship" with God and other believers is a *result* of this "life."

• *Light of fellowship* (1:5–2:29). John begins this section with the ringing affirmation that "God is light." He then takes us "into the dark" so to speak, by contrasting a variety of behaviour and attitudes with this statement about God's character. If we are truly "in the light" too, our *lives* should show it.

• *Love of fellowship* (3:1–4:21). Here John presents the difference being "in the light" should have on our relationships with one another.

• *Way to fellowship* (5:1–12). John presents Jesus Christ as the only avenue to this fellowship with God and one another.

• *Certainty of fellowship* (5:13–21). John closes his letter with a resounding statement about the certainty of salvation for those who have believed.

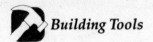 *Building Tools*

IMPORTANT PASSAGES

One of the best ways to study 1 John is to examine his use of *opposites*. John repeatedly uses "light" and "darkness," "life" and "death," and "truth" and "lying" in this letter. Make comparative lists of what he says about each. You'll be surprised and enriched at how much John has to say using the concept of opposites. (NOTE: You may also want to use a concordance to follow these same themes in his Gospel.)

KEY WORDS

know, believe, love, light, fellowship, Father, Son

2 JOHN
Truth and the Christian

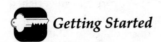 *Getting Started*

John's second and third letters provide us with snatches of insight into the mechanisms and menaces of the early church. There is evidence in these letters of a vibrant growing faith, but it is also clear that like today, they also had their difficulties. It is interesting and comforting to discover that the struggles of the early church are not significantly different than those we face today. There is much to learn in these next two "postcards" from John!

AUTHOR AND DATE

In this letter, John merely calls himself "the elder." This could refer to his age, or stature in the churches, or both. John penned this brief letter around A.D. 90 from the city of Ephesus.

FIRST READERS

The letter is addressed to "the chosen lady, and her children." More than likely she is a Christian friend of the apostle, although some feel that perhaps John is using a metaphor here to refer to a local church and its membership. The location of the first reading is not known.

PURPOSE

Apparently, a problem had developed from the normal and benevolent practice of showing hospitality to itinerant teachers and preachers. It was common in the first century for people to open their homes to those in the gospel ministry. (Jesus himself was a frequent guest of Mary and Martha in Bethany as well as Peter in Capernaum.) But it appears that some Christians were inadvertently providing this type of support to false teachers. John writes this letter to condemn that practice while upholding the principle of hospitality which is fundamental to Christianity.

THEME

Christians must love and live in God's truth, but have nothing to do with error.

KEY VERSE

"Anyone who runs ahead and does not continue in the teaching of Christ does not have God; whoever continues in the teaching has both the Father and the Son"(9).

 First Reading

The opening lines *and* the ending contain words of warm greeting, love and blessing, indicating the highly personal nature of this letter. John makes a comment near his closing that indicates the letter was perhaps composed rather hastily because he is anticipating making a visit very soon.

OVERVIEW

This brief letter is saturated with the idea of "truth":

2 JOHN: TRUTH AND THE CHRISTIAN

SALUTATION	COMMAND	WARNING	"GOODBYE"	
LOVING IN TRUTH	WALKING IN TRUTH	ABIDING IN TRUTH	JOY	
	fellowship ⟶	separation		
1	4	7	12	13

• *Loving in truth* (1–3). John shows that truth and love cannot be separated. Living together with other believers is part of growing in Christ's teaching.

• *Walking in truth* (4–6). John uses this section as an expansion of the ideas above. Living the truth out always involves our relationships with others.

• *Abiding in truth* (7–11). True believers stay with the truth. John makes a short comparison between true and false teaching and our responsibility.

• *"Good-bye"* (12–13). In his closing comments, John reminds us that true joy is the fruit of fellowship.

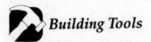 *Building Tools*

IMPORTANT PASSAGES

Although the letter is brief, you will find it helpful to follow the theme of truth through the letter.

KEY WORDS

truth, love, command, teaching, continue

3 JOHN
Soul and Body Doing Well

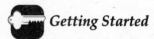 **Getting Started**

This final brief letter of John's is addressed to an individual. Although we are told his name, it is not too helpful. "Gaius" was about as common in the first century as the name "John Smith" is in many countries today! We can be certain he was *not* a Jew because Gaius is a Greek name. Like John's second letter, we again get a privileged glimpse into the relationships within the early church.

AUTHOR AND DATE

The apostle John, again christening himself as "the elder," is the author of this, the last of his three letters. John probably composed this about the same time as the other two, A.D. 90.

FIRST READERS

All that can be gleaned from the introduction to this letter is that Gaius was a "dear friend" who was loved by the aged apostle. Making lasting friends is a task that seems to become harder with age, so perhaps Gaius had been a loyal friend of John's for some years. We'll never know fully in this life the depth and extent of the relationships these mighty servants of God cultivated. But we *will* know some day, because in eternity we will have the opportunity to do the same!

PURPOSE

John's primary purpose for writing seems to be to praise Gaius for his Christian love, and identify a problem element in the church, a man named Diotrephes. It is sobering to see how openly and swiftly the early church took care of its own difficulties!

THEME

Being spiritually and bodily "healthy" means following the truth, helping others, and doing good.

KEY VERSE

"I have no greater joy than to hear that my children are walking in the truth"(4).

 First Reading

LENGTH OF BOOK

This is the shortest book of the Bible, but its message is as important as that of the longest books.

OVERVIEW

The title we have assigned this letter is "Soul and Body Doing Well." We can arrive at that from the second verse, "I pray that you may enjoy good health and that all may go well with you, even as your soul is getting along well."

3 JOHN: SOUL AND BODY DOING WELL

	reports	commendations	exhortations	
SALUTATION-1	FOLLOWING THE WAY OF TRUTH	HELPING THE BRETHREN	REJECTING EVIL AND DOING GOOD	CONCLUSION 13-15
	2	5	9 12	

• *Following the way of truth* (2–4). John is probably recalling the words of his Lord that he recorded for all time in his Gospel: "I am the way, the truth, and the life"(John 14:6).

• *Helping the brethren* (5–8). John commends Gaius for using the gift of hospitality in the *proper* way, as contrasted to its abuse in his second letter.

• *Rejecting evil and doing good* (9–12). This section contains a classic comparison between healthy and "sick" members of a fellowship.

 *Building Tools*

IMPORTANT PASSAGES

Although the letter is short, a rich study can be found by comparing the three individuals mentioned in the letter: Gaius, Diotrephes, and Demetrius. Use your imagination and try to "construct" a character profile for each.

KEY WORDS

truth, walk, good, evil

JUDE
Keeping Yourselves in God's Love

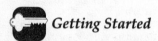 **Getting Started**

Jude's letter strongly urges Christians to be very careful not to be contaminated by the spiritual poison of evil people. As we mentioned regarding John's letters, there were false teachers and immoral persons who were secretly infiltrating Christian gatherings.[186] And Jude, prompted by the Holy Spirit of God, wrote this letter to warn his friends about this danger.

AUTHOR AND DATE

The letter opens with a statement of identity and authorship, "Jude, a servant of Jesus Christ, and a brother of James." This is undoubtedly the Jude of Matthew 13:55,[187] which would make him the half-brother of Jesus. It is interesting that Jude does not consider himself an "apostle," but only a servant of the Lord.[188] (NOTE: Two of Jesus' half-brothers wrote New Testament books; this one and the book of James.)

FIRST READERS

It is difficult to ascertain from the letter itself just who the first readers were. Jude uses the phrase "dear friends" a number of times, possibly indicating that they are Palestinian Christians because that was his "homeland." On the other hand, his letter is very similar to 2 Peter, which might indicate that his audience was the same as Peter's—Asia Minor. Whichever area it was, it appears that Jude was ministering there at the time he wrote.

PURPOSE

He wrote to warn his first readers against false teachers and

[186] see verse 4
[187] in Matthew's Gospel he is known as Judas
[188] see verses 1 and 17

252

those who have turned against Jesus. He exhorted them to remain strong in the faith and to fight actively against wrong teaching, not merely to avoid it. To Jude, the evil that was sweeping through the churches included immorality, rejection of the clear commands of God, rejection of Jesus Christ as Saviour and Lord, and an outright mockery of holy things. Jude challenges his first readers to "defend the faith"! This book is primarily a polemic against error rather than a treatise on the truth.

THEME

Christians need to be strong in the faith, and active in fighting for the truth.

KEY VERSE

"To him who is able to keep you from falling and to present you before his glorious presence without fault and with great joy" (24).

 First Reading

Jude opens the letter quickly with a short greeting and closes it with a stirring praise to God. Sandwiched between is a forceful message about false teachers.

OUTLINE

Greetings   1–2
    A. Encouragement to fight for the faith   3–4
    B. Warnings about evil people   5–16
    C. Practical advice for standing strong   17–23
Doxology or praise   24–25

OVERVIEW

Most of Jude's letter is about evil people and their sins. The middle section of the letter (5–16) is mainly Jude's *warnings*. In contrast to evil, God's truth is presented in its brightness and beauty. Jude closes his letter with   admonishment to his readers to watch their own lives and to build themselves up in the faith.

GREETING 1,2	ENCOURAGEMENT	WARNINGS ABOUT EVIL PEOPLE			ADVICE	PRAISE TO GOD 24,25
	"Fight hard for the faith."	PUNISHMENT IN THE PAST	DESCRIPTION OF EVIL PEOPLE	JUDGMENT IS COMING	"Build yourselves up"	
	3	5	8	14	17	

• *Greeting* (1–2). Jude opens his letter with words of assurance regarding his first readers' relationship with God.

• *Encouragement* (3–4). Jude gives powerful reasons why their lives should be different and why they must aggressively defend the faith.

• *Punishment in the past* (5–7). Using Old Testament history as his example, Jude reminds his first readers that God has always dealt with evil in a just and certain fashion, while protecting and rewarding the righteous.

• *Description of evil people* (8–13). Jude's description of sin and those who wallow in it is graphic and sobering.

• *Judgment is coming* (14–16). Jude makes a sweeping statement about the certainty of judgment.

• *Advice* (17–23). This is the largest section in the letter. Jude provides specific advice about what the righteous should do *for themselves* in the meantime.

• *Praise to God* (24–25). In a rousing reminder, Jude ends this letter extolling God, the source of strength and the ultimate defender of the truth.

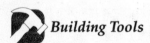 *Building Tools*

IMPORTANT PASSAGES

Examine Jude's description of false prophets in detail. List the characteristics and write out why you feel a failure to adhere to the clear truth of God results in such depraved conduct.

KEY WORDS

dear friends, remember/remind, faith, kept

REVELATION
Christ Will Win Over Evil

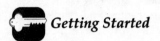 *Getting Started*

Will the human race destroy itself? What will happen in the final years of the history of the world? God is the only one with answers to such questions about the future. Many of those answers are in the final book of the New Testament, Revelation. This important book tells about judgments and blessings of the future—mainly those of the last times. Its closing chapters point to final destinies: in an eternal lake of fire called hell, or in the eternal New Jerusalem called heaven.

This book belongs to a class of biblical writings known as apocalyptic. It is the only one of its kind in the New Testament. Apocalyptic writings in the Old Testament include Daniel, Ezekiel and Zechariah. This type of literature is normally characterized by:

(1) Extensive use of symbols and visions.
(2) God's people are portrayed as *suffering* unjustly.
(3) It usually has to do with *future* events.
(4) God breaks through in the end to save his people.

AUTHOR AND DATE

The apostle John wrote Revelation, his last letter, while he was held prisoner on the island of Patmos, 35 miles off the coast of Asia Minor (see map on page 302). Tradition tells us that John was exiled here under the reign of the Roman emperor Domitian around A.D. 94.

There were three cycles of persecution during the second half of the first century. Nero's was the *first*, in the middle sixties. Domitian's was the *second*, between A.D. 84 and 96, and Trajan's was the *last*, in the late nineties.

These were perilous times for believers. They were crucified, burned alive, thrown to lions, and forced to kill one another as gladiators. And signs of corruption were beginning to appear *within* the church as well. It is into this decaying and wicked age that John is called to write this letter of God's ultimate triumph.

FIRST READERS

John clearly addressed this letter to the "seven churches of Asia," and even lists them one by one in the opening chapters. It is sobering when we see that a number of them are churches that were vibrant and healthy recipients of Peter and Paul's letters thirty years earlier! The problems and sins of these churches have universal applications, and in some ways, they stand as representative of the church of Jesus throughout time.

PURPOSE

The book of Revelation encourages Christians to stand firm amid persecution; warns them against turning away from Jesus; and calls them to be faithful. The book gives a loud and clear warning to unbelievers about the judgment of God on sin, but it also contains severe exhortations to God's people to be holy.

THEME

Revelation shows who Jesus Christ is and what his work is in the present and future. Jesus is the Head of the church, the Judge and Reward-giver of the future, and the Eternal One who will welcome faithful believers into the new heavens and earth for ever and ever.

KEY VERSE

"Look, he is coming with the clouds, and every eye will see him, even those who pierced him; all the peoples of the earth will mourn because of him. So shall it be! Amen" (1:7).

 First Reading

The book opens and closes with similar ideas and phrases, among them are the words of Jesus, "I am coming soon."[189] In between, the book deals with vivid descriptions of God's judgments on sin.

---

[189] see 1:1-8 and 22:12-21

OUTLINE
Christ Will Win Over Evil

Introduction   1:1–11
    A. Letters to seven churches and songs of praise
       1:12–5:14
    B. The future judgments of God   6:1–20:15
    C. The New Jerusalem   21:1–22:5
Closing   22:6–21

OVERVIEW
    Even though the book of Revelation is long and detailed, it consists of three main sections, each devoted to rather specific themes:

THE REVELATION OF JESUS CHRIST

CHRISTIANITY TODAY - Church -	JUDGMENTS TOMORROW - World -	GLORY FOR EVER - New Jerusalem -
LETTERS AND SONGS	SEALS - TRUMPETS - BOWLS	NEW HEAVEN AND NEW EARTH
1 setting	6 conflicts	21 victory 22

    • *Christianity today* (1:1–5:14). The seven letters of chapters 2 and 3 are about seven churches in John's day. But, they also easily describe and apply to churches of today (the "now and . . . later" of 1:19). It is comforting *and* convicting to see that the church has struggled with similar trials, temptations, and sins throughout the ages.
    • *Judgments tomorrow* (6:1–20:15). In Revelation we can read about the judgments of God as they fall upon the earth with great power: seven seals, seven angels, seven trumpets, and seven bowls. This section ends with the world's last judgments (20:7–15). The final word is "fire." We can easily see and learn from these judgments that God and his Son have complete control of world history, that they judge and punish unbelievers and that they protect the people of God who remain faithful to the end.
    • *Glory for ever* (21:1–22:21). The final point of John's vision is a happy, wonderful climax. Words like "new" and "coming"

point to heaven as a huge community of joyful saints living with their God and his Son for ever. Human words can only *suggest* what this eternal state is like. But we know that heaven is as sure as the Lord's own words, "Write this down, for these words are trustworthy and true"(21:5).

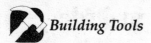 *Building Tools*

IMPORTANT PASSAGES

A profitable study awaits you in the first three chapters. Record what Jesus says about each of the seven churches regarding:

(1) What they are doing wrong
(2) What they *used* to do that was correct (where applicable)
(3) What Jesus wants them to do
(4) What can be applied to the church today
(5) What can be applied to your life, today

Examine chapter 21. Meditate on the descriptions of what eternity will be like. Write out all that you think. Then, list your thoughts on *how you should* live in light of these truths.

KEY WORDS

Two key words are repeated throughout the letter. They are "lamb"(29 times) and "throne"(44 times). The dual ideas of sacrificial atonement and God's sovereignty and judgment dominate the letter. As you read and study the book, keep a list of each occurrence of these two words and what insights you can glean from their usage.

SUPPLEMENTAL STUDY HELPS

How to Read the Old Testament Books in Order

There are different orders we may follow in reading the thirty-nine books of the Old Testament. Here are three of them.

1. *Canonical order.* This is the order we find in our Bibles, an order first established in the early centuries. Four groups of Old Testament books are involved.

   A. Law   (Genesis to Deuteronomy)
   B. History   (Joshua to Esther)
   C. Poetry   (Job to Song of Solomon)
   D. Prophecy   (Major Prophets—Isaiah to Daniel; then Minor Prophets—Hosea to Malachi)

2. *Chronological order.* This is the order based strictly on when the books were *written*. Specific dates are unknown, but the order closely follows the historical order (below).

3. *Historical order.* This follows the calendar sequence of the *settings* of the books. Refer to the chart, *Historical Coverage by the Old Testament Books*, page 287, and you will see the thirty-nine books placed according to time settings.

Historical Order of Reading the Old Testament

1. *Beginnings*
   Genesis

2. *Bondage and Flight*
   Exodus

Leviticus
Numbers
Deuteronomy

3. *Judges*
    Joshua
    Judges
    Ruth
    1, 2 Samuel

4. *Kings*
    1, 2 Kings
    1 Chronicles
    Psalms, 2 Chronicles
    Job
    Proverbs
    Ecclesiastes
    Song of Solomon
    Obadiah, Joel
    Jonah, Amos, Hosea
    Isaiah, Micah

5. *Two Exiles*
    Nahum
    Zephaniah
    Habakkuk
    Jeremiah
    Lamentations
    Daniel
    Ezekiel

6. *Restoration*
    Ezra
    Haggai
    Zechariah
    Esther
    Nehemiah
    Malachi

HISTORICAL COVERAGE by the OLD TESTAMENT BOOKS

2,000 B.C. — 1500 — 1000 — 722 — 536 — 400 B.C.

THE CREATED WORLD
Genesis 1-11

THE NATION of ISRAEL
Genesis 12 - Malachi 4

BEGINNINGS	CHOSEN NATION	BONDAGE	EXODUS	JUDGES	KINGS	2 EXILES	RESTORATION
—creation —fall —flood —scattering —nations	ABRAHAM, ISAAC, JACOB, JOSEPH		MOSES	JOSHUA	SAUL, DAVID, SOLOMON	DANIEL, EZEKIEL	NEHEMIAH, ESTHER
	Ur to Canaan	Egypt	Wilderness	return to Canaan		in Assyria and Babylon	return to Canaan

Genesis

Exodus
Leviticus
Numbers
Deuteronomy

Joshua
Judges
Ruth
1, 2 Samuel

1 Kings and 2 Kings
1 Chronicles
Psalms, 2 Chronicles
Job
Proverbs
Ecclesiastes
Song of Solomon
Obadiah, Joel
Jonah, Amos, Hosea
Isaiah, Micah

Nahum
Zephaniah
Habakkuk
Jeremiah
Lamentations
Daniel
Ezekiel

Ezra
Haggai
Zechariah
Esther
Nehemiah
Malachi

	KINGS OF ISRAEL	YEARS OF REIGN	CHARACTER	RELATIONS WITH JUDAH	DETHRONED BY	HISTORY
1	JEROBOAM	22	Bad	War		1 Kings 11:26–14:20 2 Chronicles 9:29–13:22
2	NADAB	2	Bad	War	Baasha	1 Kings 15:25-28
3	BAASHA	24	Bad	War		1 Kings 15:27–16:7 2 Chronicles 6:1-6
4	ELAH	2	Drunkard	War	Zimri	1 Kings 16:8-10
5	ZIMRI	7 days	Murderer	War	Omri	1 Kings 16:10-20
6	OMRI	12	Very Bad	War		1 Kings 16:16-27
7	AHAB	22	Exceedingly Wicked	Alliance		1 Kings 16:28–22:40 2 Chronicles 18:1-34
8	AHAZIAH	2	Bad	Peace		1 Kings 22:40, 51-53 2 Kings 1:1-17 2 Chronicles 20:35-37
9	JORAM	12	Bad	Alliance	Jehu	2 Kings 3:1-3; 9:14-25 2 Chronicles 22:5-7
10	JEHU	28	Bad	War		2 Kings 9:1–10:36 2 Chronicles 22:7-12
11	JEHOAHAZ	17	Bad	Peace		2 Kings 13:1-9
12	JEHOASH	16	Bad	War		2 Kings 13:10-25; 14:8-16 2 Chronicles 25:17-24
13	JEROBOAM II	41	Bad	Peace		2 Kings 14:23-29
14	ZECHARIAH	6 months	Bad	Peace	Shallum	2 Kings 15:8-12
15	SHALLUM	1 month	Bad	Peace	Menahem	2 Kings 15:13-15
16	MENAHEM	10	Bad	Peace		2 Kings 15:16-22
17	PEKAHIAH	2	Bad	Peace	Pekah	2 Kings 15:23-26
18	PEKAH	20	Bad	War	Hoshea	2 Kings 15:27-31 2 Chronicles 28:5-8
19	HOSHEA	9	Bad	Peace		2 Kings 17:1-41

From Irving L. Jensen, *1 Kings and 1 Chronicles (Bible Self-Study Guide)*, (Chicago: Moody Press, 1979), 108. Used by permission.

KINGS OF JUDAH	AGE BEGAN REIGNING	YEARS OF REIGN	CHARACTER	RELATIONS WITH ISRAEL	HISTORY
1 REHOBOAM	41	17	Bad	War	1 Kings 12:1–14:31 2 Chronicles 10:1–12:16
2 ABIJAM		3	Bad	War	1 Kings 15:1-8 2 Chronicles 13:1-22
3 ASA		41	Good	War	1 Kings 15:9-24 2 Chronicles 14:1–16:14
4 JEHOSHAPHAT	35	25	Good	Peace	1 Kings 22:41-50 2 Chronicles 17:1–20:37
5 JEHORAM	32	8	Bad	Peace	2 Kings 8:16-24 2 Chronicles 21:1-20
6 AHAZIAH	22	1	Bad	Alliance	2 Kings 8:25-29; 9:27-29 2 Chronicles 22:1-9
7 ATHALIAH (queen)		6	Bad	Peace	2 Kings 8:18, 25-28; 11:1-20 2 Chronicles 22:1–23:21; 24:7
8 JOASH	7	40	Good	Peace	2 Kings 11:1–12:21 2 Chronicles 22:10–24:27
9 AMAZIAH	25	29	Good	War	2 Kings 14:1-14 2 Chronicles 25:1-28
10 UZZIAH (Azariah)	16	52	Good	Peace	2 Kings 15:1-7 2 Chronicles 26:1-23
11 JOTHAM	25	16	Good	War	2 Kings 15:32-38 2 Chronicles 27:1-9
12 AHAZ	20	16	Bad	War	2 Kings 16:1-20 2 Chronicles 28:1-27
13 HEZEKIAH	25	29	Good		2 Kings 18:1–20:21 2 Chronicles 29:1–32:33
14 MANASSEH	12	55	Bad		2 Kings 21:1-18 2 Chronicles 33:1-20
15 AMON	22	2	Bad		2 Kings 21:19-23 2 Chronicles 33:21-25
16 JOSIAH	8	31	Good		2 Kings 22:1–23:30 2 Chronicles 34:1–35:27
17 JEHOAHAZ	23	3 months	Bad		2 Kings 23:31-33 2 Chronicles 36:1-4
18 JEHOIAKIM	25	11	Bad		2 Kings 23:34–24:5 2 Chronicles 36:5-7
19 JEHOIACHIN	18	3 months	Bad		2 Kings 24:6-16 2 Chronicles 36:8-10
20 ZEDEKIAH	21	11	Bad		2 Kings 24:17–25:7 2 Chronicles 36:11-21

From Irving L. Jensen, *1 Kings and 1 Chronicles (Bible Self-Study Guide)*, (Chicago: Moody Press, 1979), 109. Used by permission.

MINISTRIES OF THE PROPHETS,
AND OF EZRA, NEHEMIAH, AND ESTHER

Obadiah	840–825 B.C.
Joel	825-815
Jonah	785-770
Amos	765-755
Hosea	750-715
Isaiah	740-690
Micah	735-700
Nahum	650-620
Zephaniah	636-625
Habakkuk	620-610
Jeremiah	625-575
Daniel	605-530
Ezekiel	593-571
Ezra	538-457
Haggai	520-505
Zechariah	520-490
Esther	483-473
Nehemiah	445-415
Malachi	435–415

COMPARISONS OF THE FOUR MAJOR PROPHETS

	ISAIAH	JEREMIAH	EZEKIEL	DANIEL
KNOWN AS:	The Royal Prophet ——— Evangelical Prophet ——— Messianic Prophet	The Weeping Prophet ——— The Prophet of Judgment	The Prophet of Visions ——— The Prophet of the Exile ——— The Other Son of Man	The Prophet of Gentile Times
PROPHESIED TO:	Jews in Judea	Jews in Judea and in Captivity	Captive Jews in Babylon	Gentile Kings and Captive Jews
CONCERNING:	Judah and Jerusalem, Isaiah 1:1; 2:1	Judah and Nations, Jeremiah 1:5, 9-10; 2:1-2	The Whole House of Israel Ezekiel 2:3-6; 3:4-10, 17	Gentile Nations, Daniel 2:36 ff., and Israel, Daniel 9
DURING REIGNS OF:	Uzziah, Jotham, Ahaz and Hezekiah, Kings of Judah, Isaiah 1:1	Josiah, Jehoahaz, Jehoiakim, Jehoiachin, Zedekiah, Kings of Judah, Jeremiah 1:2-3	Zedekiah, King of Judah and Nebuchadnezzar, King of Babylon	Jehoiakim, Jehoiachin and Zedekiah (Kings of Judah) Nebuchadnezzar, Darius and Cyrus (Gentile Kings)
DATES B.C.:	From 739 to 692	From 627 to 574	From 593 to 559	From 605 to 536
NUMBER OF YRS. HE PROPHESIED:	47	53	34	69
PROPHET'S CALL:	Isaiah 6	Jeremiah 1:4-19	Ezekiel 1-3	———
POLITICAL CONDITION:	Judah Menaced by Syria and Israel ——— Alliance with Assyria ——— Assyria Repulsed	Hostilities with Egypt and Babylon ——— Deportation of Captives	Some Jews Captive in Babylon ——— Other Jews Still in Judea Threatened with Captivity	Jews in Babylonian Captivity
RELIGIOUS CONDITION:	Backslidden ——— Hypocritical	Revival Under Josiah ——— Much Sin and Idolatry After Josiah's Death	National Unbelief, Disobedience and Rebellion	As a Nation out of Communion with God ——— A Small Believing Remnant
HISTORICAL SETTING:	2 Kings 15-20 2 Chronicles 26-30	2 Kings 24-25	Daniel 1-6	Daniel 1-6

From Irving L. Jensen, *Jensen's Survey of the Old Testament* (Chicago: Moody Press, 1979), 389. Used by permission.

How to Read the New Testament Books in Order

There are different orders we might follow in reading the twenty-seven books of the New Testament. Three of those are:

1. *Canonical order.* This is the order we find in our Bibles. It begins with the four Gospels and Acts (history), then is followed by letters (interpretation), and ends with Revelation (prophecy).

2. *Chronological order.* This is the order based on when the books were written.

Chronological Order of Reading the New Testament

The accompanying chart shows a likely order of the original writing and appearances of the New Testament books on the public scene. Since the dates are not part of the Bible text, they are not firm as such. So various opinions are held on some dates, such as those of Mark and Galatians.

If you follow this order of reading the twenty-seven New Testament books, try to visualize the growing excitement and attention of the Christian communities during the last decades of the first century, as the scrolls began to circulate from city to city.

A CHRONOLOGICAL ORDER OF
THE WRITING OF THE NEW TESTAMENT BOOKS

BOOK	AUTHOR		PLACE WRITTEN	DATE A.D.
JAMES	James		Jerusalem	45
GALATIANS	Paul	JOURNEY EPISTLES	} Corinth	48
MARK?				
1 THESS				52
2 THESS				
1 COR			Ephesus	55
2 COR			Macedonia	
ROMANS			Corinth	56
MATTHEW	Matthew		Jerusalem?	58
LUKE	Luke		Rome	
ACTS	"			61
COLOSSIANS	Paul	PRISON EPISTLES	Rome	61
EPHESIANS				
PHILEMON				
PHILIPPIANS				
1 TIMOTHY	Paul	PASTORAL EPISTLES	Macedonia	62
TITUS			Corinth?	—
2 TIMOTHY			Rome	67
HEBREWS	?			
JUDE	Jude			
1 PETER	Peter			
2 PETER				68?
MARK	Mark			
JOHN	John		Ephesus?	85
1 JOHN				
2 JOHN				
3 JOHN				
REVELATION			Patmos	96

3. *Topical order.* This is by groups of similar subjects. For example, books stressing end times appear in a last group. Below is one suggested order. You will see that one of the four Gospels heads each group. The value of this order is *variety* (for example, you are not reading the four Gospels together).

Topical Order of Reading the New Testament

1. *The Old Testament
    Connections:*
    Matthew
    Hebrews
    James

2. *Church Beginnings:*
    Luke
    Acts
    Romans
    1 Corinthians
    2 Corinthians

3. *Church Growing:*
    Mark
    Galatians
    Ephesians
    Philippians
    Colossians
    Philemon
    1 Timothy
    Titus
    2 Timothy

4. *Last Days:*
    John
    1 John
    2 John
    3 John
    1 Thessalonians
    2 Thessalonians
    1 Peter
    2 Peter
    Jude
    Revelation

Key New Testament Passages

Genealogy of Christ	Matthew 1:1–17
Sermon on the Mount	5:3–7:27
Kingdom Parables	13:1–53
Olivet Discourse	24:1–25:46
Miracles	Mark 4:35–6:32
Jesus' Transfiguration	9:2–13
Christmas Story	Luke 2:1–20
Three Parables About Lost Things	15:1–32
Prologue	John 1:1–18
Nicodemus	3:1–21
High Priestly Prayer	17:1–26
Resurrection	20:1–31
Church Is Born	Acts 2:1–47
Saul Saved	9:1–9a
Missionary Journeys	13:1–21:17
Universal Condemnation	Romans 1:18–3:20
Justification	3:21–5:21
Holy Spirit	8:1–39
Israel	9:1–11:36
Marriage	1 Corinthians 7:1–40
Spiritual Gifts	11:2–14:40
Resurrection Body	15:1–58
Christian Giving	2 Corinthians 8:1–9:15
Faith and Law	Galatians 3:1–5:1
Christian's Armour	Ephesians 6:10–18
Christ's Emptying	Philippians 2:5–11
Heresies Exposed	Colossians 2:4–3:4
Jesus' Return	1 Thessalonians 4:13–18
Antichrist	2 Thessalonians 2:1–17
Church Officers	1 Timothy 3:1–13
Paul's Farewell	2 Timothy 4:1–22
False Teaching	Titus 1:1–16
Christ the High Priest	Hebrews 4:14–10:18
Faith	11:1–40
Faith and Trials	James 1:1–18

Suffering and Trial	1 Peter 3:13–5:11
World's Physical Dissolution	2 Peter 3:7–10
Fellowship	1 John 1:1–2:2
Antichrists	2:18–29
Letters to Seven Churches	Revelation 2:1–3:22
Final Judgment	19:1–20:15
Eternal State: New Jerusalem	21:1–22:5

Highlights of Paul's Life

Paul's conversion came at the height of his opposition to the church. Acts
9 reports the experience. How Paul and the Christian church came
together in the sovereign design of God is shown in the accompanying
diagram.

THREE PHASES OF PAUL'S LIFE

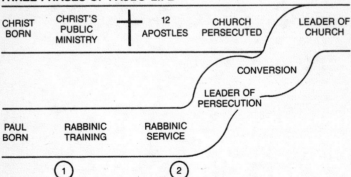

From Irving L. Jensen, *Jensen's Survey of the New Testament* (Chicago: Moody Press,
1981), 236. Used by permission.

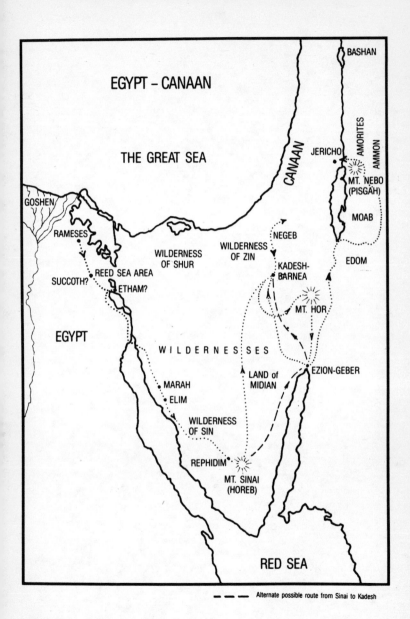

From Irving L. Jensen, *Jensen's Survey of the Old Testament* (Chicago: Moody Press, 1979), 86. Used by permission.

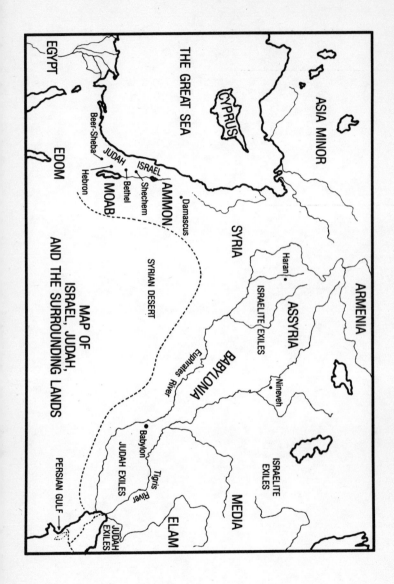

From Irving L. Jensen, *Jensen's Survey of the Old Testament* (Chicago: Moody Press, 1979), 202. Used by permission.

GEOGRAPHY OF THE MINOR PROPHETS OF JUDAH

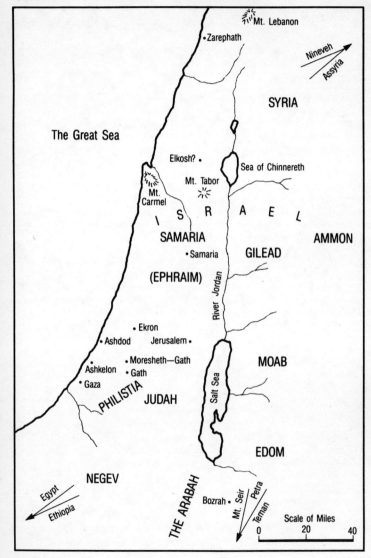

Mt. Lebanon

• Zarephath

Nineveh
Assyria

SYRIA

The Great Sea

Elkosh? •

Sea of Chinnereth

Mt. Tabor

Mt. Carmel

I S R A E L

SAMARIA

• Samaria

GILEAD

AMMON

(EPHRAIM)

River Jordan

• Ekron

• Ashdod   Jerusalem •

• Moresheth—Gath

Ashkelon   • Gath

• Gaza

PHILISTIA   JUDAH

MOAB

Salt Sea

EDOM

NEGEV

Egypt

Ethiopia

THE ARABAH

Bozrah •   Mt. Seir   Petra

Teman

Scale of Miles

0   20   40

From Irving L. Jensen, *Jensen's Survey of the Old Testament* (Chicago: Moody Press, 1979), 422. Used by permission.

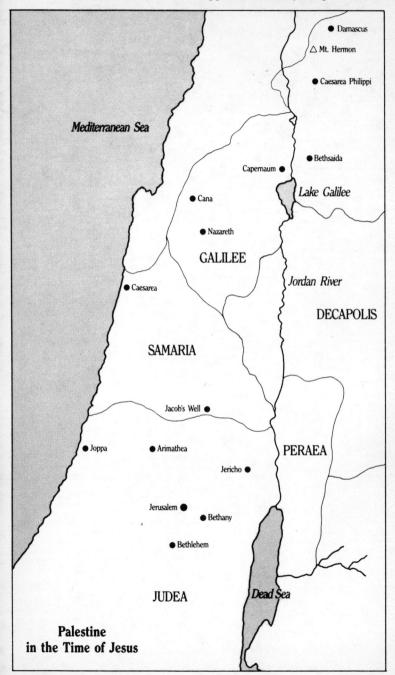

● Damascus

△ Mt. Hermon

● Caesarea Philippi

Mediterranean Sea

● Bethsaida

Capernaum ●

Lake Galilee

● Cana

● Nazareth

GALILEE

Jordan River

● Caesarea

DECAPOLIS

SAMARIA

Jacob's Well ●

● Joppa

● Arimathea

PERAEA

Jericho ●

Jerusalem ●

● Bethany

● Bethlehem

JUDEA

Dead Sea

**Palestine
in the Time of Jesus**

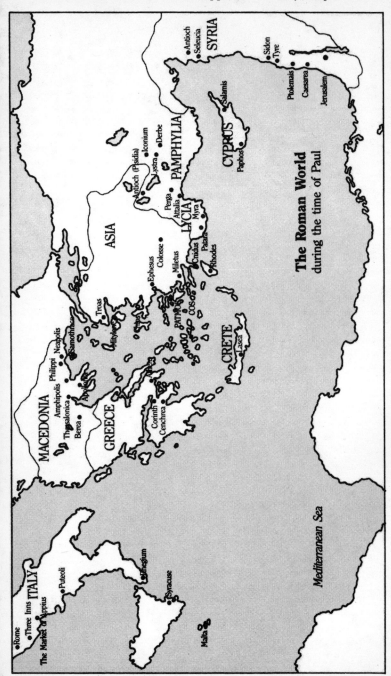

The Roman World during the time of Paul